Internal Martial Arts
Nei-gong

Cultivating Your Inner Energy to
Raise Your Martial Arts to the Next Level

Bill Bodri and John Newtson

Top Shape Publishing, LLC
1135 Terminal Way Suite 209
Reno, Nevada 89502

ISBN-13: 978-0-9721907-9-4
Library of Congress: 2011943858

DEDICATION

To the martial artist who wants to take their physical practice to the next level of greater skill, and who wants to learn the internal arts that will catapult them to a higher degree of both physical and spiritual excellence.

CONTENTS

ACKNOWLEDGMENTS

Thanks go to David Farmer for his helpful comments and quotes which we've included in the text. We would also like to thank Jeremy Antbacke, and Clairemarie Levine, for their extensive assistance in editing this text. Without their sharp eyes to catch misspellings and their push to have us rewrite certain sections, the text would be far less than what it is.

For more titles like this, please see www.MeditationExpert.com. We particularly recommend the large "Measuring Meditation" ("How to Measure and Deepen Your Spiritual Realization") for case studies of advanced cultivation practitioners at the level of Taoist Immortals.

"The Little Book of Meditation," by William Bodri, gives very detailed instructions on how to practice anapana, pranayama, mantra, sexual cultivation, witnessing meditation, and the white skeleton visualization technique. All of these meditation techniques will be useful to martial artists who wish to cultivate inner gong-fu.

You might also pick up the following related titles on Amazon.com: "The Little Book of Hercules," "Twenty-Five Doors to Meditation," "Spiritual Paths and Their Meditation Techniques," and "Tao and Longevity" by Nan Huai-Chin.

BILL BODRI and JOHN NEWTSON

1
INTRODUCTION

Recently I had lunch with a man widely considered one of the top martial artists in China. He's a drunken sword master who now teaches Kung Fu on Wudang Mountain, considered the birthplace of Taoist martial arts like Tai Chi.

I asked him, *"What are all the martial artists who failed to match your skill missing? What did you do that they did not do? Obviously, everyone who dedicates his life to martial arts trains religiously, so it cannot just be that you practiced more than they did."*

He then went into an eye-opening hour long explanation of what really made him the drunken sword master in China, and explained why in recent years there has been a great decline in Kung Fu for modern martial artists.

He said the main reason martial artists fail to develop true skill, power and ability is because they approach martial arts like athletes. They just focus on developing the external physical skills and athletic abilities, such as stronger or faster muscles, similar to how you would train in a competitive sport. They never focus on inner energy.

The problem is, the high level martial arts, especially in China, are NOT founded on purely physical skill. When he was young he reasoned, "How will I ever differentiate myself from this great crowd of highly talented and extremely athletic martial artists? If martial arts are based simply on the athletics of physical movements, then where is my chance to stand out?" Early on in his training he therefore made the decision to cultivate his inner chi energy, and to therefore practice *nei-gong* as the foundation of his art. This involved hiding some of his practice from the prying eyes of Communist officials who forbid this type of internal cultivation practice within the martial arts schools. Nevertheless, he was lucky enough that his own teacher was able to help train him by teaching him the basics.

His approach to *nei-gong* included sitting meditation, *Zhan zhuang* or "post-standing" for hours at a time (a type of standing meditation), along with breathing exercises. He credited his great skill as a martial artist directly to focusing on meditation, breathing exercises and internal cultivation. He didn't just focus on the athletics of martial arts, but on his internal chi cultivation which many today approach through breath cultivation. Cultivating your breath, such as through special breathing exercises or pranayama, is the simplest (and lowest) way to enter into this.

The reason for this book on martial arts and inner gong-fu, also known as inner energies and inner power, is because most martial artists don't know anything about how to cultivate their inner energies past a superficial stage, and there are many deep levels possible to cultivating this inner energy. This is what the traditional path of martial arts entails, and if you cultivate these energies you can do incredible things past what people even consider as the normal level of martial arts.

Unfortunately, there is no clear explanation about how martial artists can do some of the amazing, almost supernatural feats that you read about in ancient books and see represented in the movies, such as seeming to fly through the air, so I wanted to discuss why they become possible after you cultivate your energies to that deep level, and how you can cultivate those abilities yourself.

In martial arts, which are called *wushu* in Chinese, people usually start upon the path of perfecting various external forms of movement, and various postures and stances, through external exercises. This is called *wai-gong*, meaning the external martial arts. It has to do with mastering the exterior form of the body with its positions, motions and movements such as strikes, chokes and blocks. You are trying to develop body mechanics and coordination.

As people start practicing *wai-gong* they also learn how to stand motionless as well as stretch their bodies and move them in various ways, and they learn how to think in terms of strategies for attack and defense such as moving this or that way, or the positioning of the body for a certain strike or angle. The initial emphasis is on mechanics, and optimization or peak performance goals such as how to be stronger, move faster, last longer and the like.

Eventually, however, no matter how well you practice external martial arts to perfect your form, and no matter how amazing are the things you can end up doing, people usually reach some plateau for their level of skills and get stuck with this type of approach, and thus their progress eventually reaches a standstill.

To break through the plateau, many martial artists turn to breathing exercises that often deal with superficial energy streams in the body, and this type of practice is at first called *qi-gong*.

Qi-gong encompasses several different things. Primarily, *qi-gong* exercises are basically the pranayama breathing practices of India and don't extend to your internal cultivation. This is why they don't take you very far. The truest or best from of *qi-gong* practice is when you start to actually feel the chi (*qi*) in your body because of your martial arts practice, perhaps in your palms, soles of your feet, skin, or even tendons and bones. This then eventually becomes internal chi cultivation, or *nei-gong*. Prior to cultivating these internal energies, but just cultivating your external respiration with its ins and outs, this is *qi-gong*.

Many martial artists who reach a physical plateau start practicing yoga pranayama breathing exercises in order to try to open more energy channels in their body, and learn how to match the movements of this chi energy with their muscles to reach a higher skill level. Since they are trying to use the external breath to eventually cultivate internal chi that is matched with the muscles, this is going from the practice of *qi-gong* to *nei-gong*. The point is that breathing exercises can help your martial arts practice to an incredible degree.

There are endless varieties of *qi-gong*, and traditionally these *qi-gong* exercises were kept separate from the external martial arts forms and movements, and never integrated into the standard practice routines and training regimens. However, many high level martial arts experts, from their own experiments, learned how to eventually graft a *qi-gong* method onto their physical practice to activate inner energies and thus become an internal practice, but these findings were very rarely passed down in many traditions.

When you reach this stage of practicing *qi-gong* methods along with your external martial arts, you will not only begin to feel the chi of your body but sometimes you will start developing many amazing special abilities. What they turn out to be depends on the individual's natural dispositions and what he or she chooses to cultivate. Usually you are just opening up minor chi meridians in a superficial way but when you learn how to control the chi energies within your body, you can direct it to help you perform many special physical feats. When practicing the particular breathing styles of Southern Shaolin or Fukien White Crane, for instance, you must try to link certain types of chi movement with your muscular movements.

With the best level of *qi-gong* you are still at the level of the superficial sensations of chi and the superficial chi flows throughout the body, and this isn't the "real chi" of the body called "kundalini" or "yang chi" which you read about in spiritual texts that truly opens up your chi channels and chakras at a deep level. This level of practice is called "wind chi" because it is rather superficial, and not the deep life force itself. To activate this level of internal energy, which taps into the basic force behind life itself, you have to go even deeper in terms of true internal energy practice, which is called *nei-gong*.

The key principle of chi cultivation techniques are that your chi and consciousness are linked, so as you cultivate your chi you will develop changes in your state of consciousness. This is a scientific principle, and so many people cultivate their chi to calm their minds, or cultivate their minds (consciousness and thoughts) to calm their chi. It works both ways.

> Cultivating your chi is tied to cultivating the purity (emptiness) of your mind.
> Cultivating your mind (learning how to empty thoughts) is tied to cultivating both the purity and smooth circulatory flow of your chi.
>
> If your chi and its circulation can become more purified and smoother, then your consciousness can become more purified by becoming emptier (by having less thoughts).
> If your consciousness becomes emptier (has fewer thoughts and/or thought attachments), then your chi can further purify (because more chi channels will open, more channel obstructions will clear, and your chi flow will become more even, smooth, harmonious and regular).

The application of breathing exercises to martial arts is because they can affect your inner chi directly, and so they are a way to help you cultivate the chi of your body which, because this is connected with your muscles and physical form, can help you reach a new level of martial arts excellence. If you cultivate your chi you can experience the results of *qi-gong*, and then *nei-gong* in time.

When you start cultivating your body's inner energies at the level of *nei-gong*, which is the deeper step of chi practice, this finally unlocks the ability to start achieving those miraculous martial arts feats such as flying through the air and so forth which you read about in martial arts novels. This is a level where you really go deep into it and start cultivating the deepest internal energies of the body – life force itself - having used martial arts as the entry way into this, because otherwise you would never have gotten this far. You can only achieve these capabilities through a high level of internal energy cultivation.

This small book is all about entering into the cultivation of *nei-gong*, or the internal martial arts, as an entryway into those special abilities, and the pathway of cultivating (purifying) your mind because of the connection between chi and consciousness. Specifically, when you reach a point in your *nei-gong* practice that you open up the body's central energy channel meridian, called the *sushumna* in India and *zhong mai* in Chinese, and then afterwards open up the River Chariot rotation called the microcosmic circulation in Taoism, then afterwards all the body's internal energy meridians will start to open up and you can begin to enter the sphere of supernormal martial arts capabilities. Mental attachments will dissolve so that your mind becomes empty, and free of attachments to wandering thoughts, you will be able to achieve much quicker response times for your strategies and movements.

Opening up the *sushumna* central channel and other chi meridians within your body is the engine enabling this to all happen. After this accomplishment you can start inventing all sorts of special martial arts techniques and unusual abilities on your own, but only after the microcosmic and macrocosmic and other circulations have all opened. Their opening, at the level of *nei-gong*, is the minimum foundation necessary for these types of achievements. You can practice martial arts exercises to open the front and back channels of the body, but only image-free emptiness meditation can open up the *sushumna* central channel.

It would take countless books to go into this in detail, so our only goal in this book is to just introduce the topic in brief since you will find very little else in print. When you read stories of martial artists who can fly and walk through walls and move at incredible speeds - all the things that you usually see in Japanese Manga and Chinese martial arts films - that's all a product of *nei-gong* which I hope you work to achieve.

As stated, in order to do that, and get that far, there are certain things you have to cultivate and a certain level you have to reach as to the mastery of your internal energy cultivation. The practice of martial arts is an entryway to achieving this level of mastery and expertise over your internal energies, or *nei-gong*. And then once you get your internal energies to a certain stage of purification from your cultivation, *nei-gong* martial artists soon realize that there's a stage yet higher called *Tao-gong*, which is basically cultivating the Tao.

Tao-gong is totally spiritual and has to do with cultivating pure, pristine awareness without a body, unattached to chi. You slowly discover this because your mind gets progressively emptier and more pure on this path of *nei-gong* cultivation, whereupon you start to recognize that only awareness or pure consciousness is operating. A pure bodiless awareness, or pure consciousness, is the real you, and you start to get an understanding of this after you proceed sufficiently at *nei-gong*.

When you start to cultivate that as your goal, which is to experience your true nature or true Self, that's called "cultivating the Tao," or *Tao-gong*. And when you succeed at *Tao-gong*, you turn around again and complete the cultivation of the physical body to a yet higher stage than could be reached through the practice of *nei-gong* alone and its cultivation of internal energies for purely physical reasons. In Buddhism, the accomplishment of realizing the Tao is called attaining the *dharmakaya*, and then turning around to finish the transformation of your body and its chi is called cultivating the *sambhogakaya*, or Reward body of your practice.

This whole path from *wai-gong* to *qi-gong* to *nei-gong* to *Tao-gong* is actually the complete path of the real martial arts. It doesn't stay at the level where someone is just cultivating their body with external exercises, after which they can break through twenty bricks or ten boards or knock out a lot of people. You start with the external exercises, or *wai-gong*, and then you eventually start feeling your chi, *qi*, or *prana*. Sometimes this happens because of your physical practice, and sometimes because you start cultivating your breath, or breathing, in special ways. Science says your chi doesn't exist, but you soon prove it to yourself by feeling it, and then you can enter into the stage of chi cultivation with firm belief.

If you start combining breathing practices with your martial arts practice, that's *qi-gong*, and you can start cultivating your internal energies in a non-superficial way from there. You start feeling those chi energies and combining them with your muscular movements, which is at the level of cultivating *nei-gong*. Eventually you proceed to cultivating just those internal energies alone while ignoring the body, and hence we then have the higher forms of *nei-gong* which also involve cultivating pristine mental awareness without thoughts.

At the apex of martial arts, at its highest echelon, one goes from *nei-gong* to *Tao-gong*. The people who get that far, reaching these two levels, are the ones who can do all those miraculous things that you read about that are at a level above exceptional physical skill that can be cultivated, as usually seen in TV documentaries. Yes, it is possible to do those supernormal things. Yes, you can train to achieve them but you have to get to the level of *nei-gong* which requires a certain mindset, an understanding of some basic principles, and certain exercises we're about to supply.

In order to do that, in order to have those unusual super power abilities arise - and we'll get into the ways that people cultivate for that specifically - you have to, number one, open up the energy meridians in the body, known as the chi channels of the body, and totally transform your body's chi. That transformation is actually a detoxification of the physical body, as coarse and subtle poisons are expelled, and a refinement and purification of your chi. From there the emphasis moves almost entirely to a focus on further purifying the mind, although you are also cultivating your chi and body as well.

You have to absolutely open up the central channel of your inner subtle body, called the *zhong mai* in Chinese, or the *sushumna* central channel, and then the full set of internal meridians after that. Attendant with this, of course, is an initial transformation in consciousness wherein your mind becomes more open, clear, free, empty, aware and natural.

This is not a process that can be achieved instantly because to fully open up all the channels of the body and completely transform its form takes about ten to twelve years in total. That doesn't mean you won't make great strides in progress and experience amazing things until twelve years are up, but that for a first go at completely transforming all the cells, channels and so forth of the body, numerous schools cite twelve years as the common requirement for the complete circuit.

After you open up the *sushumna* central channel of the body, which kick starts these advanced transformations, in a matter of days you can eventually initiate what Taoism calls the "microcosmic circulation," or the River Chariot rotation, which is also mentioned in the Bible. All cultivation schools in the world mention this rotation of chi within the body because it exists and can be felt when it is finally initiated. The rotation is real, and often compared to the orbital movements of the planets in the sky, but you just cannot feel it until you dissolve away all the obstructions blocking your chi channels and the circulations within them. It is a phenomenon you feel whereas when the *sushumna* opens it is something you have to be shown through an inner vision. The Indian and Tibetan schools of spiritual cultivation emphasize the *sushumna's* opening whereas most other traditions, because you can actually feel the results without any self-deception, emphasize the commencement of this back and front rotation. In my view that's a better signpost or progress marker.

After this rotation opens up, you can feel the chi energies going up your spine and then down the front of your body in a circular orbit, though of course the sensation dies as those circulatory pathways are fully cleared of obstructions so that the chi circulation becomes smooth. This pathway is the *ouroboros* snake biting its tail in Greek symbolism, or "Leviathan of

Vast Face" in Judaism, and in Taoism it's the circulation of your chi up your *du mai* back channel and then down the *jen mai* of the front of your body, also known as the microcosmic circulation.

You'll find the same phenomenon mentioned in western alchemy and other spiritual schools as well, including the many tantric yoga schools of India, Buddhism, and so forth. Once that back-to-front microcosmic circulation opens up, then your chi energies can eventually open up more and more circulations throughout the body, including inside the arms, and then down to the feet. The main crux of this can happen in a matter of days once the microcosmic circulation is cleared. The full set of circulations in the body involving all the chakras, chi channels and meridian routes is called the macrocosmic circulation to reflect the larger, macro picture of all the major channels. Because these include all sorts of orbits, this is compared to the universe in general.

In Chinese Taoism, which is the origin behind many martial arts, this entire opening of the body's chi channels lays the foundation for the higher *nei-gong*, or true internal energy cultivation work. Taoism does not describe this stage of inner energy cultivation in terms of chakras, as done in India and Tibet, but in terms of energy fields and chi energy transformation. Taoism says your *jing* transforms into chi, which corresponds to your generative energies becoming chi energies that can open up meridians in your body. The fact that your muscles and cells (your entire physical nature) starts transforming is because they are made from/of *jing*.

Next chi transforms into *shen*. This doesn't mean that chi actually turns into *shen*, but that you reach the stage of cultivating *shen*, which is like cultivating clear awareness since all your thoughts have calmed down and the mental realm seems empty, vast and clear. *Shen* refers to the pristine awareness that can know thoughts, and you can rarely recognize the existence of *shen* unless you are already able to cultivate a quiet state of mind. You can cultivate a quiet state of mind because you have already cultivated your chi and opened up your channels, and so now you can pass to a higher stage of cultivation.

This stage of cultivation is very difficult to reach although it becomes easier to attain if you practice meditation techniques like "seeing the light" that are actually direct *shen* cultivation methods. In those methods you try to practice being like the light of the sun or moon in space which is clear and illuminating, present everywhere, but which you cannot see in space itself. You can only see light when it hits an object, but as to the light itself in space, you can never see its actual existence. It is invisible though always present, and only shows its power when it encounters objects. It doesn't even get dirty if it passes through dirty water but is always clean and pure. *Shen* is like the light of the sun in that it is boundless, invisible and everywhere, always present in your mind as the source of awareness, and if you practice resting in the light of pure awareness itself as a meditation practice, rather than identifying with some object of consciousness it lets you see/notice, you will be cultivating your *shen*. You can practice becoming one with it by realizing that this bodiless, empty, insubstantial but universal light of awareness is you, and you can thereby, by resting in the no-thought awareness itself, cultivate your *shen*.

If your mind is empty, without thoughts, *shen* is what allows you to know it is empty. *Shen* is not a thought or thoughts, but is the empty awareness capability shining behind thoughts that enables you to know. *Shen* allows you to know the consciousness of thoughts because it is the awareness that stands behind them. That awareness is itself empty of content, so we say it is empty. It is not anything phenomenal like chi, so we say it is insubstantial, too. It is the body of beingness without being a body of any substance, and being boundless it has no borders or shape. Because it is non-moving, too, always present even if it goes unrecognized.

The reason that you cannot recognize that *shen*, or clear awareness, is always present behind your thoughts is because you are so entangled with wandering thoughts that your consciousness, rather than the *shen*, is the only thing you know. You are fixated on the appearances within consciousness (thoughts) which obscure a recognition of the clear essence or substance of consciousness itself. Hence to cultivate *shen*, you have to practice bodiless witnessing as a third person type of detached observer.

Initially this cultivates your chi, but after you accomplish enough inner chi and channel cultivation progress, your mind will really begin to empty (quiet down) and you will eventually move to the stage where you can start to cultivate *shen* directly. If you cultivate good enough you can catch a glimpse of something like *shen* and then understand what it is, and the fact that it is always there. But until you cultivate deep mental quiet or emptiness, it is hard to realize its presence, so to get to this stage you have to learn meditation to quiet your mind and cultivate your chi. When there are no thoughts, however, with a bit of wisdom you might become able to recognize that there is an empty awareness still functioning that allows you to know the state of quiet. Realizing the existence of *shen* is sort of like a getting a sudden glimpse of something, like when you briefly catch the sight of something glistening from the corner of your eyes That empty pristine awareness without content, always shining, is *shen*. When you recognize its existence, you are cultivating *shen*, or we say cultivating the state of *shen*.

Shen is not the state of emptiness itself, which is just a stilling of thoughts. It is actually akin to the alert functioning of an empty mind. The mind has no substance or contents, and yet awareness is actively present. Awareness being present, this is why we use the word "mind." The mind is empty of thoughts, but the natural illuminating ability of the mind to be able to know things is still there functioning rather than there just being an inert, dead emptiness that cannot reflect anything. We sometimes say there is an aliveness or vibrance to it when we refer to the fact that our chi feels full at the time we realize it, for *shen* itself is empty and has no such characteristics. We say *shen* itself is empty and insubstantial, but is the invisible awareness behind thoughts that allows you to know them.

It is there when thoughts are there, and when they are not there; you can never get rid of awareness but simply never notice it. That's why you have to cultivate meditation to reach this stage of realization, for without mental quieting, which comes from meditation practice and the chi and cultivation it produces) it's practically impossible to recognize the presence of *shen*.

Shen is our always present clear awareness that you can finally recognize when you eventually cultivate your chi to a good enough level where your mind not just becomes empty, but where you can detach from your mind of thoughts (consciousness) and finally recognize that the knowing of awareness is there because of it. It's not inert emptiness, though it is empty of content, but is actually awareness itself.

Sometimes the chi channels within your sense organs, such as when using your vision in an alert state, get flooded with chi and the world temporarily seems brighter and more radiant. In such moments, when the mind is very quiet, you might get an idea of what *shen* is. This experience is sometimes called a "bright mind" because everything seems brighter. It seems as if the mind has gotten brighter and world has become larger and more vibrant because some invisible veil has been lifted, and that's when, if the mind is quiet, you might be able to recognize its ever present existence if your wisdom is high enough and you are attentive.

When it seems as if the senses become more crisp, or take on a more vivid intensity, this is because of better chi flow together with a quiet mind rather than that the awareness essence itself becomes more clear (for the clearness of awareness is pure and unchanging and can never itself become more pure; it can only become *not obscured*). In any case, that's when one might realize the presence of their *shen*. At that time, one might finally gain an understanding that there is something clear and lucid which stands behind thoughts, which stands behind the knowing of consciousness but doesn't drop into consciousness. At other times, you never seem to notice its presence. Its existence remains hidden even though it is always there behind all your knowing states. The fact that it is stationary, non-moving and always empty and clear while present explains why humans rarely realize it. Nevertheless, it is always there as an empty clarity witnessing that recognizes the mind.

Shen is not an extra lucidity or radiance of the mind which comes about through an increase in chi or anything like that. If your wisdom is high enough, you might even realize the existence of *shen* without any prior type of special cultivation. That radiance or brightness of awareness is already there, but it is during moments of "bright mind" that you might especially get an opportunity to realize it.

In short, the underlying bright mind of awareness is always clear and does not become more clear, more crisp or more intense. The essence of that awareness is always clear and never becomes more clear itself. It is the objects of awareness that are unclear - our mental states themselves are unclear – and that jumble of confusion must drop away so that we can realize its presence. We constantly fixate upon and get mixed up with unclear states of consciousness, which is why we can rarely get a glimpse of the ever present underlying awareness that lets us know them.

Shen is not a physical substance, like chi, but is awareness itself. When we experience a seemingly extra clarity of a "bright mind," this is often due to the quieting of the mind, which required a previous state of chi cultivation so that all the chi channels filled with chi and the chi flow became smooth and even. Whenever vision seems more pristine, for instance, it is often because of a unity of your vision channels having become engorged with chi and your mental states having become empty. It is not that your factor, functioning, essence or nature of mental awareness itself has actually increased in clarity or clearness. Its nature never changes, and it is only that you can only notice its presence/existence during moments or periods of what seems like an exceptionally clear mind due to prior chi and mental cultivation. Hence it is said, "when falseness departs, the true underlying clarity is revealed." The characteristics (emptiness and clarity) of awareness itself, which is *shen*, never change and its emptiness never changes either.

You must understand this. The clarity or clearness of awareness does not becomes more clear because it always is 100% clear, and it's just the objects of awareness, or consciousness, which are especially unclear due to the overlay of thoughts and mental clinging. This is why you meditate. You don't know what awareness is because you never realize you are using it; you never turn awareness to notice itself, which is the functioning essence of the mind that is absent of contents and is not made up of a substance.

In any case, at some special times people often get a chance to recognize the existence of their *shen*, and that recognition is a sort of spiritual awakening. The world seems brighter, but that seemingly extra clarity is due to mental emptiness and physical effects rather than *shen*. However, at that time you might be able to recognize what awareness is, and that awareness transcending thoughts, which is empty but lets you know, is what you want to cultivate to get to the next stage of attainment. It is the awareness that allows you to know thoughts.

In Taoism they say that chi transmutes into *shen*, or chi transforms into *shen*. It is not that your chi actually transforms into *shen* as a physical type of transformation such as we would find in chemistry. It is that by cultivating high enough, you can eventually reach an understanding of the presence of the always present clear awareness behind thoughts, which we sometimes call *shen*. Then you can switch to *shen* cultivation. Prior to this, you're not clear enough to be able to recognize what awareness really is or that there is a clear state of clarity behind the knowing of thoughts. Now you can understand it's there, which is a realization, so we say you realize the existence of *shen*. It is not like you actually see it because how can awareness see itself? It is not a physical thing or phenomena that you can see with awareness but is the awareness itself, or pure consciousness. Thus, "realizing *shen*" means understanding what it is and the fact that it is there prepositionally behind all mental states.

You can only arrive at this realization of *shen* because of prior work at meditation, or if you are really young and healthy and there's an opportune situation where all your channels are open, your chi flows smoothly and your mind is relatively relaxed, empty and clear. Meditation allows you to pass through the stages of chi channel openings and chi cultivation produced by meditation that prepare you for being like this permanently, which in turn produces a quiet mind. If your wisdom is high enough, during a quiet mind absent of thoughts you might be able to recognize its existence. Hence, chi does not actually turn into *shen*. The idea of transformation, that "chi transforms into *shen*," is only a colloquially way of speaking to indicate that you get to a new stage of spiritual practice wherein you can notice the awareness that transcends thoughts. The idea of chi transmuting into *shen* means moving from the stages of chi cultivation to the stage of cultivating this awareness which you can only now know exists because of all that prior cultivation work.

You can detach from thoughts, so you see them. To see them you must be beyond them. What stands beyond them, or transcends them, is called *shen* in some schools, transcending awareness in other schools, or illumination, illuminant, clear light of the mind, or clarity in others. It is not yet the pristine awareness of your original nature without pollution, (let's call that *awareness as being)*, but is getting closer to that.

When you meditate, your mind eventually becomes quiet and empty and your chi flow begins to circulate smoothly throughout your body due to the relationship between chi and consciousness. As your chi purifies your consciousness also purifies, so your mind becomes empty (thoughts die down) because its internal flow is no longer anywhere hampered or obstructed. During that state you can realize emptiness, or having no thoughts, but by what means do you know this state of silence or quiet?

Through the empty awareness power that stands behind thoughts, consciousness, or mind. The knower of the mind is just an empty witness that does not interfere in anything or come into the realm of consciousness. You just couldn't recognize *shen* prior to this (you couldn't know it was there as the awareness principle in the mind) because you were always so involved in clinging to thoughts and entangled with consciousness. You were always looking at something in front of you, so-to-speak, rather than trying to understand what was functioning behind the knowing. With thoughts gone, now is your chance to possibly recognize its existence in the background as what they appear in. With an opening in thoughts you get a chance to realize what *shen* is, so we say you get a chance to realize *shen*.

The clear awareness that emerges through the practice of witnessing without attachment, is *shen*. If you introspect when your mind is quiet and wonder how you can know, you can discover that a clear awareness exists from behind, and that recognition emerges as if it has been hidden within a mountain of thoughts, and thus we say *shen* is born. You also see it has always been there, but you always missed its presence and now, because thoughts die down (because your chi cultivation reached a sufficient stage of perfection due to meditation), you can realize its presence.

After the stage of realizing *shen,* you have a chance at realizing true mental emptiness and start cultivating genuine samadhi attainments. In this stage of emptiness, there are no thoughts anymore because you are just cultivating *shen* itself. You cultivate *shen* by resting in *shen* and eschewing thoughts, and since it is empty and absent of content, you can reach a true state of no thought or emptiness when you do this. We call this a state of no thought, or no mind, and it represents a state of attainment.

The sequence is the following. You cultivate your mind and body to purify your chi and mind; you thereby detach from your body and mind because of the purity you cultivate; you eventually realize what awareness is and become stabilized in awareness; after stabilization in awareness, further things will happen as your mind expands into boundlessness.

The cultivation of awareness alone, which is to become stabilized in pure consciousness, is still not the Tao. It is still not enlightenment, but just a state where awareness is still active but just aware of awareness. Awareness becomes the object of awareness, which is itself absent of content, so thoughts truly drop out at this stage. Prior to this stage, emptiness or empty mind meant a stilling of thoughts, but in this stage they really and truly drop out to become non-existent. No thoughts are existent in consciousness because awareness is just absorbed with itself, and so it is a state of non-knowing. Awareness still shines, but there is nothing to know because there are no thoughts. Awareness has turned to focus on itself. Since no objects are there, the observer drops out, too. If there isn't an observer, this means one realizes the state of "no self" or selflessness. One can eventually this way reach the Tao of enlightenment, or self-realization.

By further cultivating this emptiness (empty mind or the bodiless awareness of pure consciousness without an object), you can eventually realize the Tao, which is your original nature or true Self. Cultivating emptiness at this stage means detachment from the state of no thoughts (where thoughts seem to be absent but awareness still exists) to make further progress. So once you start attaining a realization of emptiness, you keep cultivating the emptiness of the mind, which is its inherent nature, until you realize the full Tao.

Buddhism just calls that whole process of inner energy cultivation which this entails the transformation and purification of the five elements of the physical body, which is what you're doing with martial arts if you do it correctly. It's really a process of detoxifying your inner chi channels of occlusions and obstructions and purifying your chi and channels to reach a stage of purification and internal harmony of your inner energies. Taoism says you are cultivating your chi and channels. The esoteric yoga schools say you are cultivating your chi, channels and special *bindu* points like chakra locations or other spots on/in the body. Buddhism just says you are purifying your five elements, and harmonizing your physical nature. It calls the whole process prior to cultivating *shen* something different so that you don't get attached to your physical body, chi, channels or the process.

You basically just let go of the body, and let go of thoughts, and they will die out. As they die out your chi will purify, and your mind progressively becomes more clear. As thoughts die away, the thoughts of being the body or a self die away, which is the Taoist state of cultivating *shen* and emptiness. Through this route you eventually reach a state of no self, but this is not yet true enlightenment because there is still the problem of phenomena. As one gradually cultivates a recognition of the fact that phenomena are empty awareness, too, one eventually travels the road where they can find their true self, or original nature.

This is one way in which martial arts differ from ordinary exercise, like weightlifting or tennis, where there's no spiritual component or internal energetic component of cultivating the life force of your body to its deepest and highest levels of excellence with all the capabilities those entail.

As you do this you get healthier and younger, whereas with most Western sports and athletics you just get older. Unlike western sports, the martial arts route helps you stay young and fit well into your elder years, and particularly so if you travel the road of *nei-gong* that leads to *Tao-gong*, and possibly spiritual enlightenment. This is something that western athletics and competitive sports cannot claim.

If you do martial arts correctly according to the right principles, then your chi channels will start to open naturally. But you have to turn to certain *nei-gong* exercises to start cultivating your deep internal energies, and once the internal circulation of the River Chariot rotation commences you'll feel that circulation continue for years. It'll become more subtle, and it will deepen as time goes by, opening new areas and finer chi channels within the body as it proceeds. That's the entryway into these special paranormal abilities if you continue cultivating your *wai-gong* along with this inner effort. The *wai-gong* effort helps you become healthy to prepare you for internal cultivation, and if you continue cultivating both together, there's almost no limit to what you can achieve.

That's the genuine progression of martial arts to their highest potential, which starts from external martial arts, to chi martial arts, to the internal martial arts of deep inner energies cultivation, and then *Tao-gong*. The many details to these stages are described in "**The Little Book of Hercules**" and in Master Nan Huai Chin's book, "**Tao and Longevity**," but that's an introduction for the martial arts path in general.

2
THE TWO BASIC APPROACHES

One of the issues about the training in martial arts that seems very relevant to this is that a lot of the martial arts training and practices can be grouped into two huge categories. One would be a Buddhist martial arts focus, such as for the Shaolin school and so on, that came out of the Buddhist tradition in terms of the underlying culture and mindset. On the other hand, you would also have a Taoist martial arts approach, such as found in Tai Chi Chuan, Ba Gua Zhang, Liu He Ba Fa, Aikido, and Hsing-Yi.

Of course, these traditions overlap and the division is artificial, so you really cannot say that view X (or approach X) belongs to this tradition and view Z (or methodology and approach Z) belongs to the other tradition. You also cannot say that this or that exercise or form of martial arts belongs to this group and has no origins in the other. Over time many different approaches have borrowed from one another and become somewhat integrated.

What I am saying is that there are two different approaches to cultivating your internal energies that can be summarized by referencing two schools – Buddhism and Taoism. We can make a distinction between how you approach the cultivation of the body and its energies by referencing these two schools. So, when it comes to cultivating your internal energies to reach the heights of martial arts greatness, there are the same two basic approaches summarized by the terms of Buddhism and Taoism, and there is also a difference in the explanations and terminology used in martial arts approaches that represents this different focus.

There are a lot of differences between the viewpoints of Buddhism and Taoism and how that has become reflected in the martial arts. Even so, these two schools have somewhat converged and combined over the centuries where in many cases the approaches are the same, and there isn't any difference between the two schools at all. There are always commonalities and overlaps between diverse traditions, and adepts from one tradition always sought out schooling from the other, combining the two and refining what they learned to produce the many schools and techniques and approaches we have today. This is an admirable trait, and something you should also do.

If you end up cultivating correctly in either school, which means either "approach," you'll end up cultivating your body's internal energies. But if you look at the traditions of these two schools and their two approaches to inner energies, then you can understand why it is said that there is a basic difference in philosophy between them.

Taoism, for instance, from its earliest stages, has always been about how to cultivate a human physical body so that the physical body doesn't have to die but can live forever. The emphasis within Taoism has always been about immortality – how to produce an immortal physical body, rather than an immortal spiritual body. Many branches of Hinduism focus on an immortal spiritual body, which is an emphasis in Christianity as well even though people don't explicitly say so. The idea of dying and going to heaven, to experience everlasting happiness, entails a spiritual body that does not perish.

With longevity to the extent of immortality as the objective, and the fact that life extension always involves diet, exercise, and ridding oneself of sickness, the Chinese Taoists have always been trying to discover exercises, herbs, minerals, foods, diets, routines ... basically anything that an individual might cultivate that could help transform his human body to a higher stage of perfection. Taoists would see the planets in the Heavens which have orbits that seemingly last forever, and would look at the nature of gold that doesn't rust or tarnish and also seems to last forever. Then they would ask, "How can I cultivate the energies in the human body and supplement them so that they frictionlessly circulate forever as in these examples of nature?"

Along these lines, they reasoned, "Since gold lasts forever, is it possible that all of the physiological functions of the human body could be transformed into a nature like that of gold which does not decay?" As an explanation of just one of their many approaches to pursuing physical immortality, they would research how you might use the components of certain plants to try to transform pure gold into liquid form, and then might gradually ingest it so that it could be slowly absorbed into the body. I've collected books from ancient India and Tibet with all sorts of such secret recipes and many other things just to research all the strange approaches people would take for things like this, as this pursuit and the scientific findings that came out of it were the earliest beginning of ancient science in various cultures.

After a long period of time, ingesting formulas like this would indeed transform all of the physiological functions of the body, for better or worse, just as happens when we ingest vitamin-mineral-nutritional-herbal supplements today on a daily basis. This was a perfect example of trying to use external products – rather than external martial arts exercises - to transform one's inner energies. The external martial arts approach was another route they took because done correctly, in time this would help open up the body's channels so that they would be free of obstructions, like the orbits of the planets that occur in an empty, starry filled sky.

The early Taoists would also experience the rotation of the chi within their bodies, which they'd compare to the orbits of the planets. They would also reason that the physical body passes away whereas the orbits of celestial bodies last forever, so how might they supplement these internal rotations so that they could become frictionless and never cease?

That type of reasoning, and the subsequent research, became the basis of many Taoist approaches to cultivating internal energies that are only experienced at the highest levels of martial arts. Taoists would try all sorts of things, and their many approaches became the basis of the theory of Taoist internal martial arts. As my teacher once wrote in "The Story of Chinese Taoism,"

> The circulation through the front and back chi channels [*jen mai* and *du mai*] forces coordination with the theory of the Heavenly Stems and Earthly Branches in the illustrations and numerology of the *Book of Changes*. This is known as making one microcosmic orbit (also called turning the water wheel). Later, all those who explained how to turn from the microcosmic orbit to the macrocosmic orbit and coordinate the green dragon, white tiger, lead, mercury, *yin*, *yang*, etc., the most mysterious of the mysterious, the most spiritual of the spiritual, and who aspired to be Immortals without exception, brought forth an unsurpassed alchemical method that they diligently cultivated. In the end they verified cultivation by means of reversal (the male sexual organ was contracted, and the breasts of females were restored to being like those of a young girl). A further step was attaining the ability to transform *chi* into spirit (*shen*), sending the *yang* spirit out, and having the spirit wander outside the body. This was the achievement of the golden immortal.

> There were many methods that had very great influence. Generally speaking, the views and terminology of opening the governor and conception channels and "being possessed" that were held by the renowned martial artists of the Southern School (internal) and Northern School (external), practitioners of *qi-gong*, those who focused on quiet sitting and nourishing health, and the individuals described in martial arts novels, were all derived from the theories, terms and methods of this sect of alchemy.

Basically, the early Taoists realized that you can go along with nature, and then supplement nature wherever it's possible, to lengthen a life span. Along the way, they discovered many scientific principles that helped transform the body, too, and of course they discovered the existence of the body's internal energies because many of the avenues they investigated led to this same common intersection. This discovery of the body's internal energy meridians, and the chi flow among them, became the basis of many positions and movement practices within the martial arts just as happened with the development of yoga.

A lot of the philosophy of Tai Chi and other martial arts follows a deep strategy of basically going along with nature, such as following the flow of these natural internal energies (or using an opponent's energies against him), and cultivating those forces so they do not diminish or encounter obstructions to their flow, or even trying to supplement them. This directly ties into the *nei-gong* stage where you're cultivating the internal energies of your body.

The Taoists wanted to know how to transform their bodies so that they might live forever, so once you tap into those energies, the question arises how you can use those energies specifically to cultivate the body? What exercises might you do, in line with those energies, to keep healthy or even to defend yourself in martial arts?

The Buddhist martial arts came about through different origins with a different objective and mindset. Typically people trace the origins of Buddhist martial arts to the Shaolin Temple where the Indian Zen master Bodhidharma taught the monks how to strengthen their bodies through tendon exercises, though of course there are other origins as well. These exercises developed into the art, Yi Jin Jing. I've personally seen how just one year of practicing these exercises can literally transform even elderly people's bodies from weak and sickly to strong and vigorous. I personally consider one year of Yi Jin Jing practice worth more than several years of yoga stretching.

Shaolin has a long tradition of martial arts which primarily starts from this time. At that time, there were inactive monks who were meditating all day long at Shaolin and they were pretty sickly, the story goes, because they weren't exercising but just sitting there all day. You would compare them to the bookworms of today or computer addicts who don't move.

They would be compared to couch potatoes who get out of shape and become overweight, but in this case the vegetarian monks didn't have enough food to become fat, but were sitting there meditating all day without exercising. In short, there was a tendency to become sickly and weak.

You have to be healthy to get the Tao, so Bodhidharma basically started to teach them the tendon stretches and other methods for making the body healthy. These monks forgot the fact that even Shakyamuni Buddha was well known for his martial arts skills before he took up his path to enlightenment, and you can read about his martial arts capabilities in the stories about how he met his wife and got married.

If you just cultivate meditation all the time and you don't exercise the body, it's possible to reach stages of emptiness and what's called the *dharmakaya*, which means realizing your original nature or true Self – a primordial empty base awareness that is our real being and the basis of the mind - but that doesn't fully transform the physical body. It (your chi and channels) will have indeed transformed to a certain extent, because otherwise you could not reach high spiritual states and attain enlightenment in the first place, but attaining enlightenment doesn't necessarily transform the body's internal energies and its chi, channels and chakras all the way to the extent that you can fly through the air, walk through mountains, move with the speed of wind, and so forth. That requires further cultivation!

As the Zen master Han Shan said, "It is easy to set foot in the thicket of brambles, but it is hard to transform the body under the curtain in the bright moonlight." You can realize the inherent emptiness of your true being, but even so, it's hard to transform this physical body even though it is not your true Self.

The Tao School is all about transforming this physical body of ours, as is done in martial arts, so Taoists want that achievement because it enables them to become healthy and live a long life. The emphasis in Buddhism is not on cultivating your physical body, however, because it is not the real you but just a vehicle for infinite pure consciousness to be able to manifest, and hence Buddhists ignore it to search for a direct experiential realization of the source of body, mind and the universe to become enlightened. But after enlightenment, what then? There's still a body there, which is your vehicle for living and accomplishing good works in the world. You don't want to be sick but healthy, do you not?

According to Buddhism, after self-realization you can work on cultivating your physical body until its nature becomes like pure energy because the greater, superior, primary objective of attaining the Tao has first been realized. So many masters first put all their efforts into attaining enlightenment and then go into retreat to transform their bodies. This work at transforming their body, which is essentially what the Taoists aim to do from the start, as their primary focus, is called perfecting the *sambhogakaya* or Reward Body in Buddhism. The purification work of cultivating the physical body, and realizing the Reward Body or *sambhogakaya*, has many stages. At the initial stages it pertains to clearing all of your physical body's channels and chakras, which rejuvenates the body or gives it "new life." Then it can perform all those wonderful capabilities we read about in ancient stories of martial artists with physical special abilities. But Buddhism never starts out focusing on the objective of cultivating the body, where Taoism does.

Buddhism emphasizes the mind, and only after you attain the right view of the mind being empty and the basis of all things, and the fact that spiritual cultivation has to do with the mind rather than the physical body (whose changes come along free during the ride), only then can you throw a lot of your time, energies and efforts into cultivating the body. Otherwise your emphasis will be misplaced because you have the wrong view, and your cultivation will tend to go astray because of focusing on the body alone.

Buddhism therefore says: first cultivate the mind, recognize your original nature of bodiless pure pristine awareness – the *dharmakaya* – by detaching from your physical body and even your inner energy body (or subtle chi body or whatever you want to call it). After that achievement of self-realization, only then is it safe to work on transforming your body and cultivating the internal energies as an objective in itself because if you concentrate on that from the start, you will miss the ultimate achievement of *dharmakaya* realization. You'll miss the primary achievement because of a misplaced emphasis that stole all your practice time, and you most probably won't end up cultivating the physical body to the necessary state of excellence either!

The Taoists start from an opposite angle and say, first let me cultivate the body to a state of perfection, and from that I'll end up cultivating my chi, and thereby consciousness, and get the Tao that way. I'll cultivate the body, get healthy, and then it won't cause any obstructions to my spiritual practice. I'll activate the internal energies within me, and by mastering non-clinging while they arise I will eventually cultivate *Tao-gong* and find my true nature, and then I'll have both pearls in my hand.

The Taoist approach produces individuals like the flying Immortal Lu Chunyang (Lu Dongbin), founder of the Eight Immortals Swordplay style, who had to be awakened to enlightenment by a Zen master, and the Buddhist approach produces individuals like Milarepa or Chi Kung who cultivated realization and awakened, and then had all sorts of special abilities like the famous Taoist Immortal martial artists. Most people studying martial arts don't know anything about these dual roads, so I'm trying to make this clear.

The difference between the two schools or approaches is summarized by sayings from Taoism and Buddhism. The Fifth Patriarch of the Zen school said to the Sixth, "If you don't cultivate a realization of your original nature, all your cultivation work is in vain." After one attains realization of one's original nature, or *dharmakaya*, then Buddhism stresses the completion of the *sambhogakaya*, or transforming the physical nature along with a body of pure awareness illumination.

Taoism says, "Cultivation of physical alchemy without the cultivation the realization of your absolute nature is the first error of practice. However, if one only cultivates realization of your original nature and does not cultivate inner alchemy, then it will be difficult to realize sagehood even in ten thousand eons."

One of these schools of martial arts came from this tradition or approach of cultivating emptiness first as the primary focus, which means cultivating an empty mind. You can also cultivate the physical body as well, simultaneously, to accompany that so as to keep the body fit and healthy. It's common sense and there's nothing against this, but you throw most of your focus into mental cultivation to purify the mind and investigate the ultimate origins of consciousness rather than cultivate physical exercises all day long.

The difference comes down to emphasis, degree and type of work. You basically meditate, you start watching your thoughts and they calm down and your mind empties naturally. To keep in shape, you also exercise, and in this case the best type of exercise is martial arts rather than the more static yoga, but you don't overly focus on it. Your goal, rather, is enlightenment.

The practice of meditation that should accompany martial arts is that simple, but people don't want to put the time into doing it because they think it's boring, so other methods get around to the same end result using different principles, such as visualization practice where you concentrate on an image until your mind empties of wandering thoughts except for the image. After you reach a state of stability through visualization practice, it means the miscellaneous monkey thoughts in the mind have died down, the internal dialogue has quieted, and then you are supposed to abandon that stable image you've cultivated to experience the empty mind. You try to visualize an image until it becomes stable in the mind, and when that happens, you let go of holding on to it. That's called visualization practice or one-pointedness practice because you need to cultivate one-pointed concentration to succeed on this route. When you cultivate an empty mind through this route, your real yang chi can come up and open your channels, which typically happens when thoughts seem to be largely absent.

The other approach to martial arts comes from the tradition of cultivating the body directly rather than the mind. You cultivate the body first and then later the mind, or both simultaneously with more of an emphasis on mastering the physical nature and cultivating its energies. This is the route of the normal martial artist who knows nothing about meditation, or the ideas of *qi-gong, nei-gong* and *Tao-gong*. So the doorway is either of the body or the mind.

Of these two, actually the road of cultivating the mind (consciousness) is quicker and more efficient and has produced the most successes for the target of self-realization AND cultivation of the physical body to its utmost excellence. But that's another issue entirely. Of those two traditions, both of them have people who definitely succeed in attaining the highest target, which is the Tao of enlightenment and physical excellence. You can approach it either way, but to succeed on the physical road of transformations you need an exceptional teacher.

Being perfectly honest about it, you'd have to lean more towards the Buddhist approach to find the largest number of individuals who actually succeeded in the Tao, and yet many of them used the Taoist approach of cultivating their body as the foundation, and then turned to Mind-only cultivation after they found this lacking. As for the people who actually succeeded in transforming the body from the standpoint of Taoism, unless they cultivated the same principles of pure undifferentiated consciousness and empty awareness mind found in Buddhism - since they are non-denominational rather than religious or sectarian principles - they usually did not succeed with that as well.

People get this idea that these principles of emphasis are all sectarian but they are just principles of science, such as the principles of weight lifting. Whether you are Buddhist or Taoist, Asian or Western, man or woman, young or old, Buddhist or Christian or Jewish or Moslem or whatever, if you start lifting weights then your muscles will develop to get bigger and stronger. This is a fact of science. It doesn't have anything to do with your tradition, race, culture, religion, gender, mindset, what you believe, or whatever. It's just a fact or basic scientific principle.

All the principles of internal cultivation are also principles of science and apply to all traditions, all peoples, all culture, religions, etc. in the same way. People get confused about this, but this is the case and you have to put your prejudices aside.

This fact also therefore lends credence to the principle of benchmarking wherein if you find some practice or technique in some school that is better than in another school or tradition, then you should quickly use it to make further progress. Just take the best from every tradition and put it together to help yourself make more progress. That's called innovation, and it's how the world moves forward.

It is ridiculous to be stubborn and insist one's lineage or tradition or cultural heritage is best, and refuse to adapt by incorporating skills and knowledge from other schools into one's practice. This is not the road that enables you to perfect yourself as a human being, or help elevate your tradition either, which should be one of your responsibilities if you are truly proud about your tradition. Learn from the best, use the best; just pull from the best and use the best from wherever you find it. The key is to develop the human being to its highest physical and spiritual and ethical potential, so use whatever virtuous teachings you find to do this regardless of their origins. Who cares? Prejudice is the obstacle!

In terms of the martial arts, that particular philosophy has helped develop both of those paths, the Taoist martial arts and the Buddhist martial arts. The two schools have been mixed and approaches have been borrowed from each over the long centuries. However, as a practitioner you must understand that two roads approach the cultivation of martial arts from a different emphasis, but at the very end of the day, progress is nondenominational and the stages of gong-fu people will pass through are nondenominational as well. You just have different angles available for pursuing your search for progress, and you should use what's best for you.

So for instance, a Taoist might approach their progress and practice through the idea, "Let me just start cultivating the body," and then eventually they will end up cultivating the mind. But a different mental approach, which we call Buddhist, will say, "Let me cultivate the mind to find its clear foundations and then later, as I succeed in that, cultivate the body," or "Let me cultivate the mind, with meditation as my primary focus, and the body along with it so that I stay healthy and so forth."

In Shaolin today, most of the monks are actually cultivating the body and the guts of deep meditation practice are only now returning. Because of Communism, Shaolin's situation had become materialistic, and often compared to a money making corporation wherein the spiritual focus had deviated over the last decades. However, you can still find people who really want to cultivate the mind, which is the traditional Buddhist approach, but this is difficult when you are surrounded y a primary focus on physical exercises and the body. Nevertheless, the Buddhist emphasis on cultivation to find the root source of life and the mind is slowly returning once again and meditation is becoming the main focus, as it should be.

This whole tradition was basically gutted of its spiritual content because of the Communist Cultural Revolution, but of the monks who visit my teacher in China, it's become apparent that there is an attempt at a return to the true emphasis of Zen master Bodhidharma, which was cultivation of the mind to realize one's true nature. In fact today, the leading Shaolin Kung Fu coach in China now lives and works at my teacher's center where he teaches Shaolin, Cheng Style Tai Chi and Yi Jin Jing to students, visiting meditators and anyone who cares to sit in on a class. In any case, I hope that explains some of the differences between the two approaches or types of emphasis.

The other point to realize is that in China, because the traditions have come together so much, Buddhists would talk about enlightenment or original nature in terms of "the Tao," so it's not just the Taoists who use that terminology. For the people who don't quite have a really deep understanding of the way the cultural conversation developed over this target, you must recognize that it's not just the Taoists who talk about "the Tao." This refers to enlightenment, the pathway to enlightenment, how to live in line with that pathway, and how to act after enlightenment. Buddhists would use that phrase, too, so it's very interchangeable.

If we go to India, they're using an entirely different set of words and vocabulary that mean exactly the same thing. They are just using the words "true Self" or "Parabrahman" to talk about self-realization, enlightenment, original nature, *dharmakaya*, Source nature, God, the Tao, and so on. The western religions use yet another set of vocabulary that refers to the same thing. Buddhists might say the absolute nature, or they might actually say the true Self, true nature, original nature, primordial essence, *dharmakaya*, *dharmadhatu*, etc. It's all basically referring to the same thing, and every single individual along this path, regardless of their tradition, will start experiencing the gong-fu of their chi or internal energies along this road of cultivation. The gong-fu of the path is a common, nonsectarian affair.

In short, the phenomena of *wai-gong, qi-gong, nei-gong* and *Tao-gong* are pretty universal. There are different practices and approaches found in different traditions, but similar experiences are found along the way with one of them being the supernormal physical powers you read about for Immortal martial artists. In other traditions, the Immortal martial artists might just be saints or religious figures because they didn't bundle their practices with external physical exercises and use that as an entryway into the Path. We might call them *mahasiddhas* or just yogis who practiced stretching exercises together with pranayama and meditation to realize these stages of inner gong-fu.

If we back-track, it's all basically referring to the fact that there is a primordial essence of the human being and spirit. And it's the same fundamental nature or fundamental essence for all living beings, and all matter as well. That fundamental essence has, as its natural characteristic or capability, the functioning of awareness, so it is primordial awareness or base awareness. That is why it is sometimes called pure consciousness, which has no body or content or form but is empty and therefore, free of thought. That's what pure means. And somehow that has become manifested as the individual human being and his capacity for individual consciousness or awareness, but in essence we are just this original pure empty awareness. The individual consciousness can be traced back, through cultivation (meditation), to an underlying infinite pure awareness that is the substrate of all beings.

For us as human beings within this whole universe, the key is how to find that original source of which we ultimately are "a manifestation." Some people call that original essence God, some people call it Allah, some people call it the original nature or Tao or true Self or what have you. And there are a lot of different approaches for how to realize It, and martial arts is one of those entryway approaches. That road proceeds from *wai-gong* to *qi-gong* to *nei-gong* to *Tao-gong*.

Unfortunately, most martial artists don't even know that there is this internal gong-fu side to their practice that can ultimately morph into this higher objective of Self-realization, which means realizing or becoming enlightened about their true self nature. That's because they're basically hijacked by this whole idea of being a body and the possibilities of cultivating this body. On top of that we have this heavy emphasis on calisthenics, body sculpting and weightlifting today. There's an emphasis on peak athletic performance from the field of sports psychology, and there is this inherent idea of strength training connected with bodybuilding where people are sculpting their body and want to show everyone their abs.

People think these tight muscular bodies show you are really healthy, and it certainly helps attract the opposite sex, so of course people are attracted in this direction since they have to do some development in that direction anyway. But is that really the apex demonstration of health and the highest capability of the human physical nature? It does not involve your chi, channels or chakras, so I don't think so. I don't think it can save you in a bar fight for your life either. We haven't even mentioned the fact that consciousness, morality and behavior are left out of the equation as well when we have this misplaced emphasis. With martial arts a physical cultivation emphasis of many different dimensions comes together, whereas this is just cultivating the tin exterior of the body – the outer showcase of muscles.

As my teacher always says, when people do all that weightlifting and body sculpting, we might think they look great but there is hardly any chi left over to open up all their chi channels! All the chi has gone into building muscles, so there is none left over for internal alchemy and a higher stage of internal and external martial arts progress. Yet this is what people are after, so they go for mastering the external form rather than cultivating their internal energies in conjunction with external appearance.

The other thing about this is that anyone who is at all familiar with the history of the literature from traditional martial arts understands there's this idea of the "inner door" and "outer door" students. There are the students who get the outside basic forms or elements of the martial art. That's perfecting the *wai-gong* in terms of the external appearance such as the movements. However, traditionally, only a very small handful of the top level students would ever be allowed to get the inner secrets of a martial art. And in many cases, those secrets are really this domestic technology of *qi-gong* and *nei-gong* and related topics which we will soon be discussing.

These are just a few reasons why crucial knowledge of internal martial arts is not very common. A lot of the people that have been teaching martial arts in the West may have never even seen these kinds of secret teachings within their traditions, yet they exist.

Nei-gong is called the "Internal Door" or "internal alchemy," or "internal energy cultivation." And that's why I put the entire sequence of the physical changes that happen along that course in "The Little Book of

Hercules," because even in the Tao School it's not clear what the full sequence of channel openings is within the body that is cultivated in the right way. With all sorts of colorful terminology having been used in the past, it's not even clear what the transformations of chi within the body are at around the crucial stage of the River Chariot opening. It's not clear in Tibetan Buddhism, Vajrayana or tantric yoga either, which a lot of people follow, as to what a map of the seamless sequence of achievement stages entails. It's not clear in any martial arts school or tradition either – absolutely NONE.

Nevertheless, there is a nondenominational sequence of particular channel openings, in a particular order, producing specific phenomena of a special nature of a general pattern. After the chi starts rotating in the body, then there's really no need for big discussions anymore because the general pattern after that involves further stages of emptiness realization and channel openings that naturally occur without the major overt signs that arise during the initial opening described by most spiritual schools. These openings are more subtle anyway, and very difficult to describe, so they are just described by saying you must cultivate for such-and-such a period of time. This is a point where it is said deities, dakinis, Immortals, Buddhas and Bodhisattvas, dharma protectors, "Heaven" and so on will arrive to help guide you. In any case, you now have that pattern for the martial arts tradition as well as listed in "Tao and Longevity" and "The Little Book of Hercules."

People don't recognize that Hercules was the model example of the perfect martial artist of the West because of his strength, intelligence, skill and because of the great deeds he performed. He represents a different form of gong-fu than we see in Karate, Judo, Tai Chi, *wushu* and so forth, but we should still consider him a martial artist, or wrestler at the minimum. His deeds were important because the Greek ideal was to cultivate your martial abilities not just for fighting but to use them to accomplish great deeds for the world. This ties in with the Clint Eastwood lone Cowboy figure of the West who rides into town to clean it up, or the idea of the Japanese samurai or *ronin*. In China we have the same image where a lone martial artist of exceptional skill and clear mind, personal virtue and in control of his emotions, roams from here to there fighting bandits and righting wrongs.

In the old days, that was one of the inspirational or motivational images that explained why people cultivated themselves, and it still has that attraction magic today. The idea has been captured in the comic book ethos that "with great power comes great responsibility," and that responsibility is to use it to fight injustice, help the weak against the strong, and right wrongs rather than simply to pick fights or seek bloodshed or revenge.

In any case, Hercules (the martial artist) goes through the exact same sequence of physical body transformations as described in various spiritual schools, and in his story of the Twelve Labors you even find what's happening in terms of the internal energy, gong-fu, or the stages that you go through and the signs and marks that will appear along the path. So you'll even find this common martial arts sequence of internal physical transformations of the chi and channels, when someone enters into the path of *nei-gong*, in the West! You don't have to go to the East to find this description, and the funny thing is that the West has the clearest presentation of all these internal changes of all of schools one might choose from.

The big thing is that you start out in martial arts, of course, doing your physical exercises. You practice your stances, forms and techniques ... you learn all these various exercises, stretches, and body movements and they loosen and strengthen your body. That's important in laying a foundation for internal martial arts.

After doing these physical exercises for a while you can eventually begin to feel your chi, and then you start to realize there's more to it, and you enter into the stage of feeling the energies in your body. You can start to feel the chi even though science says it doesn't exist.

For example, if you practice Zhan zhuang, the post standing meditation (you can easily search online to find the basic instructions), within five minutes of practicing you'll often begin to feel your chi. If you continue practicing this method, only holding the position for as long as is comfortable - you should never force your body for the principle is to gently lengthen how long you stand based on your own body's needs – you'll begin to feel your chi as clearly as you feel the muscles in your throat when you swallow.

If you do this every day then your practice will naturally go up a level about every three months.

At that point no scientist, no doctor, no one can tell you that chi is a figment of your imagination because you start feeling it for yourself and you can read all these books from countless traditions telling you it exists, so you know who's in the wrong, and it isn't you. You know it because you can experience it and authenticate it for yourself without any possibility of error. It's not a nervous system or hormonal phenomenon that you feel or anything like that but actual chi or life force of the body that you start feeling in a definite but superficial fashion as compared to *nei-gong*.

At this level you basically are progressing with your martial arts. But then eventually, even for somebody who has been practicing for 20 or 30 years or is considered a world class expert, you will reach a plateau. Hence, how do people commonly break that plateau? When you read the histories of so many people who have founded schools and so forth, they'll tell you they went from *wai-gong* into *qi-gong* into *nei-gong*. They start with the *qi-gong*, meaning the pranayama route or simply the road of feeling sensations of chi and cultivating their breathing in a superficial manner, and then entered into meditation to **start cultivating their internal energies at a deeper level.** The initial stage of *qi-gong*, when we say you feel chi, refers more to sensations of wind in the body than feeling and/or manipulating the real chi of the physical nature.

One traditional Taoist classification, explained by B.K. Franzis in his book, "The Power of Internal Martial Arts" (Blue Snake Books, Berkeley: CA, 2007, pp. 63-64) breaks the internal chi practice into 16 parts:

1. Breathing methods.

2. Feeling, moving, transforming, and transmuting internal energies along both the descending, ascending and connecting energy channels of the body.

3. Precise body alignments to prevent the flow of chi from being blocked or dissipated – practicing these principles brings exceptionally effective biomechanical alignments.

4. Dissolving blockages of the physical, emotional and spiritual aspects of ourselves.

5. Moving energy through the main and secondary meridian channels of the body, including the energy gates.

6. Bending and stretching the body from the inside out and from the outside in along the direction of the yin and yang acupuncture meridian lines.

7. Opening and closing parts of the body's tissues (joints, muscles, soft tissues, internal organs, glands, blood vessels, cerebrospinal system and brain), as well as all the body's subtle energy anatomy.

8. Manipulating the energy of the external aura outside the body.

9. Making circles and spirals of energy inside the body, controlling the spiraling energy currents of the body, and moving chi to any part of the body at will, especially to the glands, brain, and internal organs.

10. Absorbing energy into, and projecting energy away from, any part of the body.

11. Controlling all the energies of the spine.

12. Gaining control of the left and right energy channels of the body.

13. Gaining control of the central energy channel of the body.

14. Learning to develop the capabilities and all uses of the body's lower dantien (hara or elixir/cinnabar field)

15. Learning to develop the capabilities and all uses of the body's upper and middle dantiens.

16. Connecting every part of the physical body into one unified energy.

My personal preference is to call most of this *qi-gong* practice UNTIL you actually and truly open up the *sushumna* and River Chariot (microcosmic) circulations to a deep level, which entail very specific phenomena rarely mentioned in martial arts texts, but which you can find in "Tao and Longevity" and "The Little Book of Hercules." Most spiritual traditions date the beginning of the completion stage of the path from these same achievements, so there is a tie-in between the physical and spiritual cultivation traditions when you use this identification scheme.

Most people who think they are cultivating the left, right, central, front and back channels of the body are never really doing so, even though they feel wind energies in those circulations and can match it with their movements for exceptional martial arts skills. It's still considered superficial until you get the real gong-fu past the semblance gong-fu.

If you really want to attain the higher stages, it would be best if you started meditation practice along with your *wai-gong* from the beginning. Or, just start it now rather than wait for later. Since we're talking about martial arts as a path where people are initially attracted to the *nei-gong* through the cultivation of their physical body, since they didn't know anything about meditation or it didn't hold any attraction to them, this is something they don't normally start with.

Nevertheless (and this is the case with my own teacher who gets the best martial artists visiting him all the time so that they can receive guidance on improving their practice), practitioners who want to progress further and go beyond their current level of skills need to learn meditation. They all eventually recognize that they need to start cultivating their mind through meditation, but this recognition usually comes late after they start feeling their chi and then recognize there is something to it. Meditation gives you a sure and true entryway into cultivating *nei-gong*, and then *Tao-gong*, or the Tao. It doesn't mean you drop martial arts, but you discover that there is something higher than just the external physical martial arts to pursue, and that in pursuing it, it will also help your martial arts develop to the highest possible excellence which is achievable in no other way.

Of the breathing practices that many people turn to when they finally decide to cultivate their internal energies, there are two major ways they can do this. Actually, there are many ways they can do this, but in terms of using breathing to start cultivating one's chi, there are **anapana** and **pranayama** practices.

Anapana is where you sit and meditate, and during meditation you watch or you're aware of the breathing and the energies in your body. You don't hold to your body or cling to it in any way, but you sit there in meditation witnessing your breathing and eventually expand to also knowing your internal energies and where they are. The main technique is that you always focus on just the breath until your breathing and thoughts stop, and then further practice stages, which involve anapana combined with other methods, proceed from there.

In true anapana, you always start by focusing on your respiration, and you watch the ins and outs of your breath until your breathing calms down. You focus only on your breathing and ignore everything else. Both your breathing and your thoughts will eventually slow to a halt if you do this while remaining detached and ignoring wandering thoughts. During that state of respiratory cessation and "mental emptiness," your real chi within your body will start to arise and try to open your chi channels. That's when you will start to feel heat sensations in the lower belly, but you should just ignore these things and stay in the state of external respiratory cessation co-joined with mental emptiness. Then your body can transform rather quickly. If you need to use a tiny bit of energy to stay in this state of natural breath cessation, then you can use it ever so slightly. Whatever helps to maintain that state of natural respiratory cessation, once reached, is helpful to cultivating your inner gong-fu.

There are many more advanced stages of anapana practice, and more detailed instructions can be found in "**The Little Book of Meditation.**" For instance, you can eventually enlarge your attention to also know the movement of energies within the body while simultaneously remaining focused on your breathing. When you just shine awareness on these chi energy sensations, without clinging to them, those blockages will tend to dissolve because your chi channels in the regions of your attention will tend to open. We call those energies that you feel "blockages" because you are only feeling them when your chi is hitting internal obstructions within its chi flow pattern. Therefore, that's a blockage or obstruction.

In Taoism, you have many meditations where you sit and perform an inner watching meditation of just knowing those energies/sensations, but without focusing on your external breathing. You ignore your breathing and just focus on knowing those sensations with pressureless attention or witnessing. You can also link this with anapana to produce anapana variants, but that's not the pure practice of anapana. In some of these Taoist practices you also try to see the internal organs of your body.

Taoism has countless meditation techniques involving the body. In Buddhism, you have basic meditation practice, called vipassana, in which you practice watching your thoughts without getting attached to the thought flow (which prevents losing your concentration). That mindfulness of watching your thoughts without attaching to them (and thereby losing focus) is similar to Confucian mindfulness that requires you to always watch your mind. In detaching from thoughts they will die down, your internal energies will start to circulate freely, and you will accordingly start to attain the inner gong-fu of channels opening and chi purification.

You can see there are all sorts of related meditation techniques. You can also observe the internal sensations within your body without clinging to them. In these practices you don't try to push them around or link up with them in any way. You don't try to circulate them but just know they are there. This is inner witnessing, or inner observation practice, which is another way to cultivate your chi and channels by staying aware with detachment, and letting go. You might try the practice of observing your breathing without getting lost in following other thoughts, which is the aforementioned anapana. When you practice any of these techniques correctly, all sorts of internal chi channels within you will open up and the chi flow within your body will smoothen out by itself. This, then, becomes true *nei-gong* practice, and of course there are higher stages from here.

This opening of the internal chi channels is a foundational basis for many higher martial arts attainments. For instance, when you are doing standing poses you are also hoping to open up the chi channels in your legs and thighs through a different method than in sitting meditation, but you can use the principles of meditation practice during those poses to accomplish this result all the quicker. Remain detached as if a third person observer, detach from your body and its sensations, and let go while standing in the position. Then your chi channels will open up quicker while you practice the stance posture. As an alternative to watching your thoughts, this type of muscular practice in conjunction with detached witnessing helps to cultivate your body incredibly fast. You let go of your body as it reacts, and simply aloofly witness without clinging.

Do you know what "mental clinging" actually means? If you are in front of a two lane road and notice the cars going by in both directions without being bothered, that's witnessing or watching. Let's say that all of a sudden your friends come along in a convertible with the top down, and you start watching that specific car to the exclusion of all others, and watch it go down the road while ignoring all the other cars. It captures your attention so you start following that car with particular focus and start thinking of your friends and all the things you do together. All of a sudden you forgot that you were supposed to be watching the stream of thoughts because you got all caught up in this one and your mind started to wander. You lost your concentration, and that's mental clinging or attachment. That's exactly what you should NOT do.

In anapana practice, you sit there in a meditation posture and you watch your breathing through the nostrils with non-attachment. Your inbreathing and outbreathing is what you remain focused on, and you ignore other thoughts that come by but just remain entirely focused on the breathing even if it seems boring. This is cultivating the art of concentration, or one-pointedness in focusing. This takes concentration, which is why this is a concentration practice. It means you just stay with that certain topic as the focus of your mind, and remain with it while ignoring everything else, refusing to budge by losing focus. You watch until your mind calms down, your breathing calms down, and you eventually reach a state of respiratory calming where there aren't too many thoughts anymore either. Your breathing has slowed to a halt, your thoughts are silent, and your real chi starts to arise inside you. Eventually you can witness the internal energy sensations of your body, but not initially.

This is real *qi-gong* that turns into *nei-gong*, but most *qi-gong* practitioners don't know it. You practice concentration by staying focused on the ingoing and outgoing breathing process. That's the focus of attention, so you don't want your thoughts to stray elsewhere. You just remain focused on following the breathing. That's the first step that eventually leads to internal energy cultivation, or *nei-gong*.

What happens if you just keep the attention on the breathing through your nostrils is that you are practicing one-pointedness in concentration. That's it – it's just a practice of maintaining awareness on something that is moving – namely your breathing – and we're using your breathing as the focus of attention because of a scientific principle. The particular principle used in this practice is that your breathing is linked to your chi and consciousness. If your breathing calms down then your mind will calm (thoughts will die down), and if your thoughts die down then your breathing will calm (die down). If you can eventually reach a state where both calm down together, that's when your real yang chi, or real internal energy (the Indians call it kundalini), will start to arise to open up your channels. To get to this stage, you make use of the principle of the interlinkage between chi, mind and respiratory breathing to reach a state of calming where your real yang chi starts to come up. If your mind is occupied by wandering thoughts, however, you can never reach mental cessation and respiratory cessation, so you remain focused on the breathing just as you might remain focused on a mantra during mantra recitation.

Eventually the focus can also encompass the "breath within the body," meaning your internal chi energy, as well, but then it becomes a larger practice entirely different, although still related to anapana. You always start with the respiratory breathing because at the start you cannot feel your inner chi energies. Concentrating on only your breathing process, by just witnessing it, will keep your mind focused, stationary, and prevent it from wandering. Then your thoughts will calm down and your chi will arise. Concentration is what allows your real chi, or kundalini, to come up.

In order to correctly practice anapana, you must end up letting go of your body and not cling to anything you feel within your body. When you don't cling to them, which means you aren't crimping your chi channels, then your energy channels can start to open fully, and your chi will eventually start to circulate as best it can. It doesn't happen right away but takes time to learn how to do this correctly, just as it takes time to master certain techniques of martial arts, so you shouldn't expect results instantly. The rule or principle is:

Practice Method + Diligent/Intensifying Effort + Time + Patience = Results.

If you let go of your body, you're not holding on to it. Hence all your chi can start arising in your body and opening channels because you're not holding on to any muscles or sensations that would interrupt or block that natural flow which you just allowed to happen. You just practice pure witnessing, and thus your chi channels can start to open.

This is the actual secret behind the "dissolving blockages" methods of martial arts, but very few realize this secret or its usefulness for the highest levels of martial arts attainment. By witnessing without attachment you can know where energy blockages are within your body. By shining awareness on them without grabbing, chi will run there and they will open. You can also try to dissolve blockages by releasing them with an outbreath, by practicing certain methods such as the **Six Taoist**

Healing Sounds, or by mentally offering them away. There are a lot of techniques you can try such as described in "The Little Book of Meditation."

Anapana is the highest secret of Zen school dhyana-samadhi practice, that transforms the physical body, but few know this fact. Whether for martial arts attainments or high spiritual practice, anapana helps open up the chi channels in the body, and thus helps transform the physical nature quicker than most other cultivation techniques - but not if you are pushing or holding on to your chi.

Here's the main secret. You cannot open up all the tiniest of chi channels in your physical body unless you let go of your chi by cultivating an empty mind through meditation. That detachment, which means you are not interfering with your chi, allows it to flow freely without mental entanglements that would bias its circulations through habitually used, incorrect channel routes. If you cultivate a mind of detachment that is not enforced blankness or thought suppression, then your channels will open. If you try to force them into opening, you'll always miss them as you cannot force chi into the tiniest channels. If you always use your mind in a certain way then certain behavioral patterns will form in consciousness and your body, and certain chi channel pathways, like neural pathways, will open to receive traffic while others stay relatively closed.

Hence, only by meditation, and changing your behavior, can you really open up all your channels, and become a better human being in the process. We say "better human being" because when a human being is truly virtuous, all the right channel pathways are opened. When prone to anger, greediness or other habits, other channel routes are preferred to the ones that should be opened. Naturally this ties in to the transformations of consciousness, virtue and perfected behavior, and it's a complicated process we can only begin to hint at.

Force, on the other hand, will simply shunt energies into the largest already opened pathways, which is why force, and visualization of chi orbits, is not the correct way to truly open the chi channels of the physical body. You train and practice, letting go all the while, and finally your real yang chi will arise and do what it naturally wants to do without interference. That's when it will open up all the proper channels as explained in "The Little Book of Hercules."

At some point of true *nei-gong* practice, after opening up all your major channels because you attained the true stage of macrocosmic circulation, your chi will start running through all your large channels simultaneously, and you will feel this full body circulation everywhere. It will continue to do this for years, and only slowly will you make further progress as the rotation continues. You can learn how to combine your external movements with these internal movements of chi, which is a particular way that martial artists can practice one form of *nei-gong* for higher martial arts attainments.

When people hold special yoga *asanas*, they are supposed to be holding their body in these special positions to train their chi to move through the channels more easily, but few yoga masters actually ever get to the stage where they open up their channels and feel their chi so that they can accomplish this at the level of the highest possible excellence. As a martial artist, you have the benefit of being able to cultivate an opening of your channels through your movement exercises, meditation and practices like anapana. Once awakened, you can learn how to combine those energies with your movements to reach a higher stage of physical excellence.

Anapana can help to speed the transformations which occur during this period, and so can *prajna* wisdom analysis of your mind so that you realize a higher state of emptiness whereby more channels can open. If you lose your chi through sexual dissipation during this time, naturally the force of this rotation will be reduced, but there are instances wherein sexual cultivation practices, without semen loss, can also help to open up more channels.

To more quickly progress at this level of attainment, you need to meditate to reach a higher stage of letting go, at which point a new degree of yang chi seems to arise, and it can purify even further. Even more channel routes will open from this achievement that cannot be opened in any other way. This is a time when practicing Zen and Vedanta techniques (which prompt you to detach from the body and all forms of consciousness) will really bear fruit. The *prajna* wisdom exercises of contemplating, "What was I before I was born," "Who am I?," "I am Awareness-only," "Everything I see is just my mind," and so on can help you let go of everything. Only by letting go can even more channels and chi routes in the body open. This necessitates a whole book in itself because of the complexities, so I can only give the barest of explanations as this is the stage of Tao-gong cultivation.

Progress in chi cultivation will proceed very slowly unless you continually strive to attain new stages of emptiness realization. For each breakthrough in learning how to let go of your thoughts and the body, the response will often seem like a fresh sudden yang chi arising within, but of lower intensity than earlier arisings. That new arising will open up yet more channels, although initially the new rotation may often feel slow, as if the chi seems to be moving against molasses, and this reflects the difficulties of opening up obstructions. This explains why many martial artists, and meditators, feel their energies stuck inside after a new stage of progress. At this point, sometimes non-ejaculatory sexual relations will restore a smooth circulation of chi in the channels, and help one pass to the next stage of progress.

As you proceed on cultivating higher and higher stages of letting go at higher and higher levels of refinement, you can eventually transform your entire body's set of chi channels, at which point you will be able to do almost miraculous things, as many great Buddhist monks and Taoist practitioners were said to demonstrate. This is one of the highest levels of martial arts achievements, but it also requires incredible transformations in consciousness wherein one ceases to view themselves as a body or independent self. Since chi and consciousness are linked, at these higher stages one will then start to be able to cultivate the really miraculous martial arts capabilities mentioned in ancient stories.

Therefore, if you want to attain a higher stage of practice, wherein a yet higher, more refined level of chi is reached and many more channels open, the rule is that you can only do so by cultivating a higher stage of emptiness attainment through a new level of mentally letting go of chi and consciousness. This is basically called "purifying consciousness."

The body is not you, so let go of it and its energies. You are simply pure awareness without a body, pure consciousness, and you have been holding on to the body and mind and identifying them as your Self. Consciousness is not you, but just thoughts that arise and pass by, so you learn how to let go of consciousness through meditation practice, and since chi and consciousness are linked, with each stage of letting go a new level of chi rotation can commence in your inner etheric subtle body. A new level of bright mind, or *shen*, can be reached as well because consciousness purifies as your chi purifies. The cultivation of the body and mind proceed together, step-by-step, through this route of practice.

Anapana can start you upon this road of transformations. It is a practice of watching or witnessing your breathing while letting go and refusing to attach to your thoughts. People think anapana only refers to the physical breath, but after the internal embryo breathing commences, it awakens chi flows and chi circulations within your body as well, which can only be felt at the higher, non-introductory levels of practice. This, then, becomes *nei-gong*. This higher stage is very similar to the Taoist practice of "inner viewing." If you can witness your entire body as one unity of chi, through the fruits of anapana practice and meditation, you will unite the entire chi of the body into one whole. You will feel, witness, see or realize the body as one single body of chi extending from the trunk to the arms and legs and including the head - all one single body, unified and whole. So just witnessing will enable an opening up of all the tiny chi channels that will link the body's unconnected or slightly obstructed channel orbits and produce one unified inner chi body.

This will, of course, link the energies of the upper and lower regions of the body, and so you will be able to feel them as one unity in terms of an inner chi body, which is one of the necessities in martial arts practice. It is an infallible technique for integrating the upper and lower torsos into one whole, stressed time and again in martial arts traditions. One practices in martial arts to do this with the muscles and instincts, but at this level we are talking about channels, chi and consciousness.

When people practice alternate nostril breathing pranayama, which is typically what is taught in India, they don't realize that it is meant to be pranayama-anapana practice for the entire left side of the body, from head to foot, and then the right side of the body, alternately. You breath in the left nostril and feel *the entire chi* of the left side of the body from head to foot as one whole, and observe it with witnessing to note where it is stuck, smooth or coarse so that it all links and fine channels obstructions are dissolved. Naturally, it can only be perfected after someone really opens up the left and right channels to the real level explained in "The Little Book of Hercules," but this is the basis of extremely advanced martial arts practice.

With alternate nostril breathing, after you first do this for the left side of the body, you will then do this for the right side of the body. Then you do it for the left and right sides of the body simultaneously, without linking them as a whole unity. Then you link them as a unity, then ... there are all sorts of variations, each of which discovers different obstructions that are dissolved by the awareness of mental shining and knowing.

This type of pranayama-witnessing practice can be done for the front and back of the body, alternately, and even for the body trunk and your individual arms or legs which can be sectioned into halves or quarters. It is possible to do this using a particular chakra as the center of the breathing to get the practice started. In advanced anapana practice, you first start knowing the breath going in and out of the nostrils, then you notice it in the mid-section of the nose, and finally you switch your focus to notice it at the internal bridge of the nose between the two eyebrows (Ajna chakra position) when you are more advanced. There are other variations beyond that as well.

In ordinary pranayama practice, people don't realize that when they are inhaling, exhaling and holding their breath, they should be practicing anapana at that time while remaining detached from the body and relaxing it as much as possible. This is why they never make progress using traditional Indian pranayama techniques. The different ratios of in-breath, out-breath, and holding patterns enable you to practice anapana for different periods of time and eventually, as your chi channels open, you can gain control over those energies just as you can in martial arts. But no one ever teaches pranayama practitioners the secret of the technique, which is that witnessing practice should be used together with pranayama.

In any case, anapana practice is how one discovers obstructions in the chi circulations of the body parts that would otherwise remain unnoticed unless you employed this sort of technique. Normally you only notice the larger chi route circulations and tend to cling to these because the sensations predominate. This is the quickest way to discover obstructions in tinier circulations and all sorts of chi routes not described in texts, but which definitely exist. The technique, in general, can only be truly practiced to the level of mastery after someone really opens up the left and right channels to the real level explained in "The Little Book of Hercules." Regular people who simply practice pranayama cannot do this. Nevertheless, this is why some people in India – such as Buddha's students Rahula, Ananda and Mahakasyapa - were not only able to attain the Tao but transform their bodies to those of Immortals and attain all sorts of martial arts type physical superpowers as well.

Only if you open up all the channels at extremely refined levels of chi can this happen. The highest tantric stages of this practice, are accomplished with the help of deities, and few discuss this either. When asked why he had many superpowers, Shakyamuni Buddha once replied, as part of his answer, because of the help and teachings of the deities. "Deities outside, deities inside" - only if you get to this stage of practice will you be able to realize the meaning. When one starts to cultivate *shen*, when deities are said to arrive to help teach you, the meaning of such things becomes clear. This refers to the road of the highest transformations possible for the physical nature, and of course at this level you should consider the deities great Bodhisattvas and dharma lords for the assistance they render in helping you purify and learn to control the chi circulations of channels, orbits and chakras.

As to the stage of ordinary practice below this level of achievement, in truth not much progress goes to people who practice alternate nostril breathing because they never combine their practice with meditation to cultivate an empty mind. You must combine meditation with your physical practice. The same goes for ordinary yoga practitioners. I have met countless yoga masters who started practice from age five who, in their twenties and thirties, had supple bodies but no abilities to feel any internal chi at all, and no understanding of emptiness. Furthermore, they were always complaining that their bodies were sore and with one yank you could dislocate their joints because they had stretched things too much. This is yet another set of reasons why I prefer martial arts, and mastery of chi through this route, over the path of yoga, though of course yoga is extremely helpful and commendable. It is just that people who practice yoga do not seem to ever match it with meditation or chi cultivation, which is the main reason why it was developed. As to bodies that are too supple, this is the mistake of taking things to an extreme. It is similar to the martial arts error of damaging the knee, shoulder and wrist joints from overextension or pounding exercises that aim to destroy and then rebuild the bones.

I have also met people who have spent several years in one of the three monasteries in India totally devoted to pranayama practice for hours a day. While I was extremely impressed with the many pranayama techniques combined with special yoga asana positions they showed me, which do not appear in texts, they were some of the dirtiest chi cases I have ever encountered, once again because they never matched their physical practices with meditation and true mind emptiness cultivation. You need to practice meditation to clear the dirty chi out of your channels, especially for martial artists. For instance, martial artists who hold on to their chi too tightly also tend to develop a darkened countenance, and can become cases of "dirty chi" as well.

When you practice meditation and anapana in conjunction with your martial arts gong-fu (kung-fu), you will eventually be able to feel the pulsation of the inner embryo breathing (in the lower belly) behind this macro circulation of chi in the orbits until the chi flow smoothens out and you ascend to the next level, after which you must repeat the process all over again until ultimate emptiness of the body is reached. During these processes you will also feel the breathing at various other chakras, too, as special circulations are opened. One can and should shuttle back and forth between various formless samadhi emptiness cultivations, and the still body-dependent dhyana attainments that cultivate the chi of the body, to make the most progress in this technique for transforming the body, a very high secret. There are many details and nuances to this which cannot be explained in this introductory book.

In regular life you're interfering with your chi flow circulation and blocking it all the time. Clinging to thoughts biases the proper chi circulations as well. In this practice, you're just a bodiless awareness watching your breathing, and eventually you switch to witnessing, knowing, watching, observing – however you wish to word it – the internal chi energies of your body. Sometimes they are stuck here, or moving there, or they are hot or cold, and you'll feel it, but you don't interfere with it or even try to touch it with your mind but in a detached manner just recognize it, note it, witness it. Because of that dispassion of watching without involvement, what can happen is all your chi can start opening up your chi channels.

When your chi starts to open up your internal chi channels, acupuncture meridians, energy channels, *nadis* or whatever you want to call them - every school has a different terminology for them – this is the stage of transforming the inner subtle chi body that is like a superstructure framework within your body. As these channels open up, they also open up in your muscles which thereby become softer, more flexible, free of knots and entanglements, etc. – and that's how you then begin to break your plateau and move on to a higher level of progress. As the chi opens up the muscles, they also heal of injuries and you get healthy as a byproduct of your practice.

Another way that people approach this is they turn to actual artificial pranayama physical breathing methods in themselves rather than just watching the breath and internal energies dispassionately, as a bodiless observer without a center and without attachment. The best school of breathing methods for this doesn't necessarily come from China, though of course the Chinese have developed many such techniques over the centuries. To learn the cream of these techniques, you really must turn to Mother India, and of course, to whatever is considered the cream of the cream of the top pranayama exercises found within the other different cultures of the world.

There are hundreds of pranayama breathing methods from India wherein people basically do alternate nostril breathing, with various rhythms and of various lengths of inhalation and exhalation, where they're also holding their breath. You can find many such exercises mentioned in yogic books such as the "Hatha Yoga Pradipika," although there are hundreds more. You basically breathe in one or both nostrils over a certain length of time, hold your breath for a certain period of time, and then expel it for a certain period of time.

You might be taught to expel the breath from one or both nostrils, and to expel the breath quickly or slowly, but the most important part is actually holding your breath for certain ratios or periods of time during the exercise. You also might inhale your breath while holding certain static positions or performing special movements, but these are the basics. There are so many different derivations of the main idea that the methods are countless.

Those techniques have a number of different features, but the big feature within them, as mentioned, is something called *kumbhaka*, which is a period of forced respiratory pausation where you hold your breath without straining your muscles tightly. You really want to exhale because you've used up all the oxygen in your lungs, but you don't let yourself exhale. You just keep holding your breath, which is artificial *kumbhaka*. Then, when you cannot stand it anymore, finally you let yourself exhale.

Kumbhaka is that state of forced respiratory cessation where you just hold the breath without letting it out, and this is key because during that holding period many of your chi channels are forced to open. If you can remain relaxed during that period, which means letting go of your muscles rather than holding them tightly, then many chi channels can open that will help your martial arts *gong-fu*. Thus pranayama techniques that teach you how to hold your breath are excellent preparatory *qi-gong* methods for martial arts practice.

In the higher stages of meditation, as previously mentioned, the breathing or respiration stops naturally, and there is no external in breath or out breath. Therefore *pranayama kumbhaka* practice is actually a type of preliminary training for this experience, which can only happen when someone is healthy, such as someone who has approached the Tao through the vehicle of martial arts or the path of relaxed witnessing meditation.

You don't need to have followed the path of martial arts to experience the natural state of *kumbhaka* where the cessation of breathing happens naturally without force, because you can just cultivate meditation and reach that state of pausation naturally, called *tai-hsi* in Taoism. That's the state where your internal embryo breathing, or kundalini, really starts coming up, which is a precursor to the opening of the *sushumna* and River Chariot rotation, so you want to train for that accomplishment.

The best way to train is through meditation in conjunction with pranayama, so now you know the basic practice principles and techniques and why they are done. Pranayama, or holding your breath, will help open up the blocked chi channels of your body, and that will give a boost to your martial arts practice, and also pave the road for later *qi-gong* and *nei-gong* attainments.

In pranayama techniques you learn to hold your breath for one minute, two minutes, three minutes, then four minutes, then five minutes and so on. There are a lot of people now who do **freediving** or deep sea diving. They can hold their breath for many minutes, and when you see their bodies you can feel the chi coming off because they've opened up many channels and mastered some type of concentration or mental scenario to be able to let go of their body during these periods. They really develop healthy bodies from these practices, though of course there are safer ways to learn how to hold your breath without risking your life.

If you learn how to correctly hold your breath for long periods of time, it will help your gong-fu practice as well as any type of meditation spiritual practice you're doing because it will open up all the tiny chi channels in your body. I always recommend people learn the **Tibetan nine-bottled wind** *kumbhaka* pranayama practice from the "Diamond Sow" Buddha, Vajravarahi. In this pranayama practice you inhale the air slowly through one nostril to fill your lungs as much as possible, hold your breath for as long as possible, and then exhale through the other nostril as quickly as possible. There are a lot of details to the practice which you can find on the web.

Everyone hates the practice but always benefits, and I have had quite a few people who had practiced pranayama for years tell me it's the best single pranayama technique they've ever found, and I can say the same. I have met three individuals, who all had lung tests performed, and everyone told me their doctors said their lung capacity increased more than twenty percent because of the technique. That's incredible that three separate individuals all had their lung capacity measured and were told it had increased by 20-30%! What's even more incredible was the fact they weren't even devoted practitioners of the technique, but just did it from time to time because everyone hates it.

Most of the entryways into *nei-gong* for individuals who are devoted to body cultivation practices – the martial arts, Tibetan Buddhism, yoga practices, sports and athletics - are through breathing methods to cultivate *qi-gong* first. One of the big secrets of the Vajrayana school of Tibetan Buddhism and its emphasis on transforming the physical body is that most all the preliminary techniques are based on breathing methods. Most all the wonderful gong-fu you read about, after people have been doing visualization, prostrations, mantra recitation and meditation, are actually, at their root, based on the foundation of those techniques in conjunction with breathing or chi practices.

There are a variety of practices in the world to help you step forward again and start making progress, and the entryway they all use has you eventually cultivating a superficial level of your chi which you can grab hold of through *qi-gong*. You either approach it from the standpoint of cultivating your breath, due to the connection between your internal chi and breathing (respiration), or you learn how to cultivate those chi energies directly using your mind. On this road, you cultivate stability of the mind through states of one-pointedness, at which time it will become easy to sense and feel chi energies.

When you cultivate states of one-pointedness, such as through stationary (non-moving) visualizations, for instance, you can eventually feel the chi as it starts working through the meridians in the body, and can begin to grab hold of it and move it because of the connection between chi and consciousness. The principle is that wherever your mind (thoughts or consciousness) goes, your chi will follow, so when your chi becomes free and you start moving your mind, your chi will go along with it. Focus on a bone and it will go to that bone, focus on an internal point in the body, or *bindu*, and it will go to that point. Hold your mind in one place on an image and the chi of your thoughts will be held stationary for awhile, but the chi energy of your internal physiological functions will be free of other thought interferences, and start to move. You tie up the chi of discrimination with concentration, and then you can begin to unleash and cultivate the chi of your body, and you will feel it.

These are basic principles of science and are especially used in the tantric yoga schools and Tibetan Buddhism. Many martial arts techniques emphasize these factors as well, so they are not unknown secrets. They just aren't widely known. Chi and consciousness (mind, or thoughts) are like a rider (the mind) and his horse (the chi). Wherever the rider tells the horse to go, it will go there.

The point is that you can learn to grab hold of some of your chi energies and direct them with your mind, *but initially in all martial arts and meditation practice this is never your real chi, just superficial "wind chi" energies.* That's the assumption or identification mistake most practitioners make, but they don't believe you because they can move this chi, and its description seems to fit that of yang chi. Nevertheless, it isn't the real kundalini or yang chi we call the true life force. People who make this mistake have not gotten to the higher level where their real yang chi comes up, after which they then realize that what they thought was their "real yang chi" wasn't at all.

At the beginning stages of martial arts the chi you feel is akin to wind in the body. It's just a semblance phenomenon that matches the descriptions of the real yang chi, or kundalini, but is just superficial chi, or wind chi. Once again, and this cannot be overemphasized, it resembles the real chi but is not. Even martial arts masters who can somewhat control their chi make this mistake because they haven't gotten to the real stage of *nei-gong* chi cultivation!

Most people in these routes get lost after they become able to manipulate the wind chi of the body in various ways and think this is the real thing, but the real yang chi never comes up until after you open up your root chakra and your real yang chi, known as kundalini, opens up your central channel and the River Chariot circulations and you have a painful full body kundalini awakening, called the Big Knife Wind in Buddhism. Even after that it takes a long while for the real yang chi to fully arise and transform all the cells of your body. You never get to the real stage of cultivating *nei-gong* until you reach this level of opening the great energy meridians inside you, and not reaching this phenomenon you will spend years playing with the wind chi.

This is why Buddhism never emphasizes these phenomena from the start, as shown in "The Little Book of Hercules" and "Tao and Longevity," because people always think this is the Tao, the real way of cultivation, but it's so far away it's ridiculous. This is just learning how to manipulate the superficial wind chi of the body, but since you can get some results from this and certainly feel it, you can't dislodge these people from this notion. Even if you can grab hold of the real yang chi of the body, this is a type of physical cultivation that tries to bring consciousness into the body when the real you is everywhere, so it is mistakenly connected with the idea that the body is the real you.

This is why Buddhism doesn't teach people to cultivate this until after they've "seen the Tao" and realize that the body is not their true self, and all the various body energies are not their true self or the way to cultivate the realization of their original nature, or true Self. Only after they know the correct view and understand the correct path can they take this road of cultivating their body directly, but Taoists always get lost and start spinning their wind chi energies and play with these things all day long. At the end of their lives, they never get anywhere and have to start all over again next time. They don't extend their longevity or reach the real level of martial arts we are talking about along this route when we mention *nei-gong*, but they think they have, so hardly anyone can develop the super powers of someone like the Tibetan Milarepa who could fly and have body doubles and perform all sorts of miraculous transformations.

Once again, you can only develop those real abilities when you reach that level and go far past the opening of the *sushumna* and microcosmic and full macrocosmic circulations. You need to be cultivating some degree of empty mind to do so.

In any case, this is how and why in brief you can start upon a road to break your plateau and reach a new level of martial arts skills and excellence by doing breathing practices.

3

CORE PRACTICES FOR DEVELOPING INNER POWER: ANAPANA, PRANAYAMA AND VISUALIZATION

Most martial artists who have done some kind of breathing exercises generally were told to start by counting their breaths. This counting is not really necessary, but is just a device to get you to actually start practicing the task of following your breathing and to keep your mind on the practice rather than wandering everywhere else in distraction. The target is to stop wandering thoughts, and therefore if you are told to count your breaths, then you end up paying attention to the counting. You thereby ignore wandering thoughts, which can then finally quiet down due to the lack of attention. With thoughts quieting down, and your breathing calming down, the two calming down simultaneously will lead to your chi and consciousness calming, and hence you have the recipe for cultivating mental emptiness as your breathing slows. It's as simple as that. We are simply using breathing as the focus of attention rather than some other moving process.

The "necessity" for counting the breaths doesn't exist. It is an expedient method to just get people started at this type of meditation exercise and help them concentrate on the witnessing of the breathing process without wandering. Some people have a great ability to concentrate on one thing for a long period of time, so if your mind doesn't wander or waver too much, you don't have to count. You only need to keep watching the breath without letting the mind roam elsewhere, so if you are good at concentration then forgo the counting. And in the watching of your respiration, you should not be putting energy into muscles or get caught up in body sensations and somehow connect them with you, but just witness everything as if you were a bodiless observer, a universal awareness without a body that simply chooses to watch the breath of this body until it calms down and you realize an emptier mind that has fewer random thoughts running around.

Here's how to practice - just relax right now and close your eyes and let go of your body. Loosen your belt, take off your watch, sit in a cross-legged position or upright in a chair, and relax. There should be nothing tight constricting your body so that you can generally ignore it. You're going to concentrate on your respiration, watching your breathing without force, and this will cultivate your ability to concentrate. You just notice, you observe, you witness - that's a better word - you witness that the breath is going in and out of your nostrils. You also feel your internal breathing. That's it. There's nothing else you have to do. Just keep your mind on your breathing through a long or short inhalation. If your mind starts to stray from following the breathing, just bring it back to notice the doings of your breathing at that present moment.

It's hard to keep to that sort of concentration, but if you keep your mind on your breathing to the exclusion of all else, both your breathing and your thoughts will die down, and you'll enter into the *nei-gong* stage of practice where your internal energies start to become activated. You will reach a state of mental quiet, and it's during that state/time that your real yang chi will start to arise to open your channels. That's what you want.

This is anapana practice. You don't try to move your chi. You don't try to smoothen or control the chi in your body. You just notice your breathing, it calms down, you eventually realize a relatively empty state of mind, your yang chi comes up while the mind is empty of thoughts, and further chi and channel transformations proceed onwards from here. When they occur, you witness them along with the breathing. You are simply using the breathing process as your mental focus to reach a state of mental calming, which leads to *nei-gong* transformations.

Later you can pass to a more advanced type of anapana where you watch your breathing and also feel chi energy in your body by noticing them with your awareness. That's called "knowing." In some places your chi might feel stuck, so you know that fact. In other places it might feel a little warm, or wettish, or coldish, and you notice all those things within the body felt as one big empty sack. Just noticing obstructions in a region will tend to help open the chi channels in that region and smoothen things out, but you do not – I repeat – do not have to try to smoothen things or move your chi in any way. Just remain focused on knowing your breathing and your internal energies as one big whole that you watch with dispassion. You'll notice lots of internal sensations but just know they are there within the body as one wholeness. That's called "shining" awareness on body sensations because you don't cling or use force. If you continue following your breath while exercising this larger knowing of internal sensations, too, and feeling all the inner chi of the body as one whole, that's a higher stage of anapana.

When you start doing this, eventually you will notice energy moving or existent in an area. It's awareness that lets you notice anything, and that bodiless awareness that doesn't grab on to anything and doesn't cling but is just invisible, effortless, empty, and just allows you to know. If you settle for a minute or so, you'll feel stuff in your body. You might feel dull or stuck in certain regions. You might feel the outline of your body. You might feel energy in your body. You just notice it without getting involved in any other way other than to know it's there by witnessing it, recognizing its existence there. Period. You don't try to move anything. The awareness doesn't move, but you remain aware of things that do move without getting sucked in and then moving your mind. You try to notice them and the breathing while being a bodiless observer so that you can feel the entire body as a whole, and your awareness stays independent and detached.

When you notice your chi, the more you can let go of holding on to it and notice it, the more it will become able to naturally open up all the chi channels in a region because you aren't interfering with it. Eventually the channel meridians will open if you just watch without interference. The more you let go of your chi everywhere, while noticing its movements or sensations, the less you're crimping it in any place, and the more the chi in one particular region can connect with all the chi in another region by linking up with it through the opening of obstructed chi channels. Your chi channels will simply open.

This is the best analogy I can provide that will help you practice correctly and make progress. From this practice you'll basically be able to let the real yang chi in your body finally awaken, by clearing away all the layers of clinging obstruction that stand in its way, and then your real kundalini will arise. It all involves not attaching to consciousness (body sensations or thoughts) but resting in the clear awareness of knowing that does not cling. Then all these chi transformations will com about, and you'll be on your way to genuine inner gong-fu.

What happens when the real yang chi in your body arises is the following: it arises from your root chakra, goes up to the top of your head through the *du mai* channel in your back, and then comes down again through the *jen mai* or chi channel in the front of the body. Then from there all sorts of other chi events will happen and other phenomena will arise.

Much of this progress depends upon maintaining a degree of celibacy so that you don't lose your *"jing* elixir,"* so to speak, and you must let go of holding on to consciousness and the chi of your body. During this witnessing of your breathing practice, or witnessing of internal energies, you must let go of body sensations and never hold your muscles tight; as you make progress you will proceed to a witnessing state of your internal chi energies and actually feel something along those lines. If you can do that, then the chi energies within you will automatically open up what's supposed to be opened up in your body in terms of the correct chi channels and chakras in the correct, natural order. You don't have to guide anything as some Taoists suggest. In fact, you must do the exact opposite – just let everything go and see what happens, and just witness it. You don't really know what should happen, so you just witness it.

When you walk around, you can see a lot of martial artists who look really athletic or tight, but they don't have a lot of chi. What they have cultivated are muscles and strength, but not necessarily their life force chi or inner power. They have chosen the route of athleticism by cultivating their physical muscles and physique rather than the route of cultivating internal energy through meditation.

The route of cultivating one's inner energy, however, is what our Wudang drunken sword master had realized would separate him from the crowd, and indeed it made him an exceptional martial artist. All it took, he told me, was doing the same sort of simple chi practices over and over again while holding nothing in his mind. He was cultivating his chi while also cultivating emptiness meditation.

You can sometimes see people in regular life whose faces are full of energy, and they're always very happy and their minds seem empty in the sense of not-clinging very much. Therefore their chi, because they're not holding on to it, has basically opened up their channels to some degree. That's why their faces seem full, for the chi rises into the head.

If those people sit in meditation, and if they meditate for a long period of devoted practice time, eventually the root chakra will open up and they will get the beginnings of all this progress – and they didn't need to travel the road of martial arts to do this. However, the benefit of cultivating the martial arts and meditation at the same time is that you can quicken your progress in both these dimensions by combining the practices.

For martial artists, because they've already worked on the muscles, it means they've already been doing a lot of body cultivation, and they have probably already opened up some channels from this work. If they are really healthy - because martial arts are supposed to improve your state of health - they can start feeling the chi in their bodies, whereas ordinary people who don't practice normally cannot feel anything; they have what we call "dead' or "dumb" bodies. This type of inner witnessing practice will help open up their channels even more and get them to a higher level of practice. If you do this practice well, you really, really will start opening up your chi channels at the stage of *qi-gong*, which is pretty rare since most people never get these instructions. Eventually your true yang chi will arise and start to open up all the other channels as well.

When that happens you will start to experience various purification phenomena, and the chi channels that run across the whole course of your body, throughout your muscles, will start to change. At first these changes will involve a superficial degree of channels, but eventually, if the *sushumna* opens, you can start opening up all the major and minor meridians in the body – which is the entire macrocosmic circulation. It all starts from this simple sort of practice applied diligently, but during this practice you need to relax your muscles and not hold them tight. After they transform, your muscles will be relaxed and soft when you don't need to use them, and when you need to use them they'll be hard and strengthened instantly. They don't have to be hard all the time, which is losing energy.

Another method that people use for cultivating *nei-gong* is **visualization practice**. My teacher told me the story of one martial artist in China who was very famous. He used just one simple visualization practice, which was the white bone skeleton meditation technique. He basically visualized that his whole body was just a white skeleton without flesh, and when he stabilized that visualization (which cultivated all of the chi and chi channels along the entire extent of his body where the bones reach) he would afterwards release that image to experience a mind like empty space. The skeleton then would become dust in his imagination, and it would blow away, so that he just experienced empty space, or thoughtlessness, and then he would rest in that. In other words, he practiced concentrating on a visual image to settle his thoughts, and then he let go of even that image to experience an empty mind.

From just that one practice, nothing else, he was able to develop such agility in his body that this martial artist could jump six or seven feet high, or even jump from the ground to a roof. He could turn his head almost 180 degrees because the muscles became so soft and flexible. He got all sorts of other super powers as well. One time, someone broke into his room while he was sleeping, and he just rolled over and pointed a finger at him, and the man froze in that position until morning. There are a lot of stories about this guy and his martial arts abilities. My teacher met him when he was very young, and asked this famous martial artist, "What did you do?" He said, "I just cultivated this one single technique, the white skeleton visualization, and nothing else. I never even practiced special *wushu*. That's it."

The visualization technique works through a different method than anapana, or even pranayama where you hold your breath. The practice of *kumbhaka* pranayama basically forces your body to try to pry open some chi channels when you refuse to inhale again to bring in more oxygen. The Tibetan nine-bottled wind practice is the best single pranayama technique you can add to your martial arts routine for this route.

Anapana (attention placed on the breathing), on the other hand, cultivates detached concentration so that you eventually arrive at an empty state of mind because through dispassionate witnessing your channels open and your thoughts calm down. During that empty state of mind, your real chi will arise to open up your chi channels. After countless channels have been opened and you start to feel internal energies, you can then practice another technique of just being aware of them without attachment so that the chi flows harmonize and the channels all open. This is the higher stage of anapana practice when you become a more advanced practitioner. Past this stage your breathing stops and you remain aware during that state, experiencing an empty mind like space and yet knowing all the internal sensations of the body such as channel openings and chi flows. This is when you start entering into the cultivation of samadhi-dhyana. Those are the stages that produce superpowers.

The reason visualization practice works to produce mental calming is that when you visualize something and finally produce a stable visualization, within that stable visualization mindset all the extraneous thoughts of your mind are gone because you have been concentrating on just that one stable visualization. There's just one mental image you are holding onto. Your mind becomes focused or concentrated on that one internal visual image, and so you end up ignoring all the other wandering thoughts that might arise to distract you and take you into another topic altogether. It's a method of producing emptiness by banishing wandering thoughts.

If you visualize an apple successfully, there are not one thousand other thoughts going through your mind. You're not thinking, "What am I going to do tonight for dinner?" "What am I wearing tomorrow for work?" There are not all these other thoughts that race through your mind. You're just trying to visualize that one image, so you end up ignoring all these other potential thoughts. The problem is holding that image for a long time without getting sucked away into these other thoughts that come and go, and that's why this becomes "concentration" practice. When you get good at it – because you can't do it immediately unless you practice – you can hold an image with some stability and very few random thoughts will still be running around in your head, at least not as many as previously. This is how you cultivate an empty mind, which is also in some special cases therefore called a state of concentration.

Visualization practices are particularly useful for individuals with very busy minds who are addicted to thinking and cannot stop. You end up using thinking against itself by holding your thoughts to forming one visualized image. It enables you to reach a state of mental stability where there are not a lot of wandering thoughts. Because there's just one thought (the visualization), when you let go of that visualization then your mind can be empty because all the other thoughts that usually run around are already gone. They are not there anymore, and now the visualization is gone, so nothing is left. In that state of empty mind, which is like empty space, all your chi can start arising and open up all the body's chi channels or energy meridians. So it's a very effective practice for some people, and for others not so. You never know until you try.

Anapana in particular, and this type of practice, are typically used by people who have very, very busy minds because you have to tie up the mind to keep it from wandering. What a lot of people don't realize is that the white skeleton visualization involves your skeleton, which runs the whole course of your body, and that's why it's such a great practice. All your chi channels run along its course!

Since it forces you to study the human anatomy, visualization is a great practice for martial artists who are always trying to memorize acupuncture points for striking, or what the Indians call *marma* points, and other critical body regions. As stated, the martial arts should be combined with traditional oriental medical knowledge, particularly from the schools of China and India, and this requires a physical and energetic knowledge of the body. Of course, the martial arts purpose of striking involves destructive objectives, such as "how can I disarm this opponent or kill them or incapacitate them in the quickest possible way?"

The equivalents to the white skeleton visualization practice are some of the tantras that you see in India or Tibet where you're told to visualize that you're a Buddha and that there are various chakras in your body. In the white skeleton visualization you visualize all the bones already within your body; you can look at a limb and visualize the bones within it. An alternative is to also just perform a visualization in your head without connecting it to your body, but the more established way is to just visualize the bones within you, and so you end up visualizing that your body just becomes a white skeleton sitting there.

The tantric yoga visualizations from India involving all of the body's chi channels and chakras are essentially the same type of practice, but people get so lost in these practices and never dissect them scientifically that they tend to fall into superstition and develop strange mystical ideas. Therefore, I don't like to recommend them except for the "Six Yogas of Naropa" commentary by Tsong Khapa, which is an excellent book to study. There is a special subset of chi channels and chakras within the body that he instructs you to visualize with stability, and that is the basic tantric visualization for helping to learn concentration, mental quieting, and therefore the opening of your internal chi channels. As Tsong Khapa explained, the main visualization in the "Six Yogas of Naropa" is the basis of the body heat yoga, which in Chinese terms simply means the arousal of kundalini or yang chi.

To understand this technique, first you must understand that all of the systems of highest yoga tantra visualization involve envisioning the body's left and right chi channels, and then using breathing methods (or imagined internal energy methods) to redirect those energies into the *sushumna* central channel to open it. This is different than Chinese meditation where the focus is on emptiness cultivation to open up the back and front channels, and then letting the left and right channels and *sushumna* sequentially open naturally. The Chinese approach this from a more effortless tradition whereas the Tibetan methods, originating from yogic traditions, usually involve some application of active force.

In many of the Tibetan methods, which were based on tantric yoga techniques originating from India, the practitioner focuses on the navel chakra with breath work, mantra practice and visualization practices that use the AH-sound. This is how the practitioners hope to open up and draw energies into the central channel. These practitioners feel that if you don't cultivate the body's chi and channels, but simply cultivate emptiness (an empty mind), they cannot get the highest stages of progress. This explains the advice of Milarepa to he scholar practitioner Gampopa. Milarepa said to him, "You cannot get oil by crushing sand. The practice of samadhi is not sufficient in and of itself. You should learn my system of inner heat yoga, which redirects the subtle life-sustaining energies into the *AH-*stroke mantric syllable." Hence, the inner heat doctrines of Tibetan yoga focus on arousing the kundalini energies and trying to coax them in the central channel through force, whereas in China this is just approached more naturally because of the Buddhist and Taoist traditions of naturalness and effortlessness.

Tibetans call their particular practice technology the "inner heat vehicle," and this inner heat simply refers to the kundalini or frictional feelings of the yang chi as it opens up chi channels. If a practitioner can open their channels enough to establish a good foundational basis of practice, they can then practice sexual cultivation with a consort, or *karmamudra*, to also help transform the body.

The basic practice of the inner heat yoga is to sit in a cross-legged meditation posture, and hold the tongue up against the upper palate of the mouth with lips and teeth closed. The hands remain in the standard meditation posture, placed just under the navel, although I have found that in some cases it may help to rest them on the knees or lap with special finger mudras. The neck slightly bends forward and the eyes are always relaxed during the practice, either closed or cast downwards looking towards the nose.

Next one starts to visualize their internal chi channels, namely the left (*lalana*), right (*rasana*) and central channel (*sushumna* or *avadhuti*). You start by envisioning the central channel, or *sushumna*, four fingerwidths below the navel at the center of the body (not in the spine but *in front of the spine*). You visualize that the three channels rise into the head, supporting the chakras like pillars. This is just an imagination to entice chi into these regions after extended concentration, so whether the picture is entirely accurate or not is irrelevant.

Here is the most important point. You envision that the lower ends or tips of the left and right channels curve up into the base of the central channel because you are hoping that your efforts will draw their energies into the base of the *sushumna*. By making this connection through visualization, you are hoping to produce this specific result, so it does not matter that the channels actually continue downwards and even come to the tip of the penis in a man and to the vagina in a woman. Above the central channel rises on through the top of the head to the point between the eyebrows, which is why this is a common focus point for meditation, and the two side channels come to the inner passages of the two nostrils.

When envisioning the channels, there is no set rule for visualizing them as having a certain sized diameter, but it is often said that thinner is usually better than larger because it requires more concentration, or we can say that when you can steadily envision thinner diameters for the channels, it shows that your concentration abilities are improving. The best rule is to *use what works;* size is unimportant. As to colors, when focusing on the central channel alone in various types of tantric visualization, it is usually envisioned as the color of a burning flame. For this particular visualization method for the inner heat yoga, you imagine that the right channel is red, the left channel is white and the central channel is bluish in color.

Here are the visualization practices for the four chakras along the *sushumna* starting with the navel chakra.

In the belly around three fingerwidths below the navel (the precise location beneath the belly button is not as important as the general region of just below the belly button internally) is the navel chakra called "the wheel of emanation." For this method the shape is assumed to be somewhat triangular, like the (Sanskrit) syllable *EH*, and it has sixty-four petals which are red in color and stretch upward. This conflicts with the shape reported in many classical accounts, which is circular, so one might alternatively use that instead; the details of its shape are not particularly important because all you are trying to do, when visualizing it, is loosen the channels in the general region of the belly so that the chi can become more free and proceed upward. This is why you focus on the color red and channels that extend upward, and in many traditions a triangle is always used to indicate the commencement point of ascending chi energies.

The fullness of this chi awakening is often felt everywhere in the belly when practicing other meditation techniques, which is why the belly often gets warm all over even from mantra recitation practice (which shows the channels are starting to open), and this explains why a large number of channels are mentioned.

Once again, do not get overly concerned with the shape, number of petals, or even the colors of chakras, as these are all expedient instructions used to help you focus your attention. Some instructions simply work better than others, and that's why they eventually become a traditional technique like a pattern set in martial arts. You simply want the chi in this general vicinity to loosen and the chi to thereby start ascending upward, and so you practice a particular visualization upon an area. This actually is accomplished naturally through normal meditation practice when you meditate correctly, but here you are actually trying to speed the process, or so goes the traditional yogic thinking. You are trying to establish a steady mind through visualization practice, and in focusing upon a region, bring chi to that region as well to loosen chi channels in the vicinity. This makes use of the principle that wherever your mind will go, you chi will tend to follow.

At the heart chakra, which is known as "the wheel of truth" or "dharma chakra," the shape is said to be somewhat circular. It is said to have eight major petals (branches), which is why you often see mandalas with eight Buddhas arranged in a circle, or nine section square (the center section represents the *sushumna*), used for visualization purposes. These pictures, such as found in Shintoism, are meant as supports for visualization practice in conjunction with visualization/chi exercises for opening up the heart chakra just as we are trying to do here.

At the throat is "the wheel of enjoyment" chakra which is also envisioned as being somewhat circular in shape. Once again, the exact anatomical description of these chakras is never being transmitted in these methods, but a particular methodology was simply invented that proved to be effective, and that method was used to help bring about the intended effect of the opening of the channels in that area. When there are a bundle of channels in an area, as the nexus of a branching out distribution system, that is called a knot or chakra location. The more channels there are in a region, the harder it is to open them all evenly although of course this happens in time after the main circulations open and clear out.

In some schools the throat chakra is said to have twelve petals and in others sixteen. For this particular tradition of the inner heat yoga, sixteen petals are used in the visualization. In truth, the actual number is of absolutely no importance or consequence but you must decide upon one number for the purpose of creating a stable visualization. In this system the throat chakra is visualized as being red in color with the petals stretching upwards, while in many other systems the petals are visualized as pointing downwards. This has to do with the fact that we are trying to get the chi to ascend with this technique, and after a full chi circulation is established, the chi will of course both ascend and descend through this region, ascending prominently up the spine through the *du mai* and descending through the front *jen mai* channel, which accounts for the downwards descriptions. If this particular method of inner heat yoga said that the channels were pointed downwards, it might confuse practitioners who are trying to form a stable visualization.

There are also chi flows through the left and right side channels and other channels that criss cross through this region, but they are ignored for the purposes of this practice which are to simply get things going, and then afterwards you don't need this visualization technique anymore. In fact, after your major meridians are opened you rarely practice such things any longer but simply practice anapana for samadhi. They are simply a training vehicle used to get you to a certain level of achievement. In any case, there are many different glands and structures in this region with complicated circulatory pathways, which is why the throat chakra is said to be particularly difficult to open. You can therefore see that all these visualization components are simply expedient means for concentration practice, and do not accurately represent the colors or anatomy of the chakras with their branches.

The crown chakra, visualized at the top of the head, is known as "the wheel of great ecstasy." In this system it is visualized as somewhat triangular in shape with multi-colored petals extending downward, thirty-two in number, inside the center of the skull. In some schools this number is increased to one hundred or even one thousand petals. In most schools this chakra is most often visualized as round and golden in color within the head. In Taoism one often reads accounts that that the chi going through the crown chakras causes a melting of golden elixir from around the petals which drips down the head. In Buddhism the petals are symbolically represented in several different ways, such as by the little curly cues of hair on a Buddha's crown. Nearly all the various descriptions you find of the opening of the crown chakra related in various traditions are usually due to fictional visions provided to practitioners to signify progress and let them know that region is somewhat opening, and mean nothing in themselves.

In trying to visualize the chakras to a point of stability, two factors are important: the relative placement or location of the chakras (i.e. you make sure you visualize the throat chakra in the throat, the heart chakra behind the breastbone about two to three fingerwidths up from its base, etc.) and the radiant appearance of the images. The images should be lucid and bright, and in a relatively correct position to loosen the chi channels in that approximate region.

Because it is said that we want to open the *sushumna* channel, the most important focus of attention should be in the lower region where the three channels join. As to the rest of the practice, one visualizes the four chakras, with the number of petals mentioned, and fixes their mind on the images to eventually create a state of mental stability, or one-pointed concentration. It takes time and persistence to master the ability to form a stable visualization, so this type of visualization technique for *nei-gong* internal energy cultivation, namely the opening of channels, takes devoted practice. With persistence, one can develop increasingly better visualization abilities to form clearer pictures in one's mind.

If, after lots of practice effort, you cannot achieve any clarity when trying to form stable mental images of the chakras and channels together, one should try to concentrate on visualizing just the three channels. In this case you should especially try to focus on the region above (right around) the heart chakra, which is just behind the breastbone located in the center of the chest (not at the location of the physical heart).

If you cannot do this well, and cannot reach some state of stable mental clarity, you should then try to form a stable visualization inside you of where the three channels join in the lower part of the body. The belly, for this tradition of practice, is focus location of attention, rather than the perineum. (One must be careful not to spend too much time focusing on the lower regions because it might overly stimulate sexual desires and lead to adverse effects on the kidneys and the small and large intestines.) In this inner heat yoga tradition, one also tries to first establish clarity in holding a radiant appearance of the channels and chakras for a prolonged period of time.

In my personal opinion, the truth of the matter with these types of visualization is that you are just learning to hold your mind stable, which normally leads to chi channel openings, rather than the practice results being entirely due to prolonged visualizations on a chakra point that brings chi to the area. The key to the practice is the ability to hold a stable visualization, and thereby develop a quiet mind, during the practice. From that mental quiet, your chi will start to move and your chi channels will open as they do with all meditation methods that cultivate a stable quiet mind.

From the extreme of yin, yang always arises, and you can cultivate a stable visualization to get that yin state of silence, emptiness, stability/concentration, or just cultivate an empty mind directly. The visualization route just happens to appear more active than standard forms of emptiness meditation in tying up thoughts, and yet other methods equally accomplish the same result of decreasing wandering thoughts, such as anapana. The resulting stability of mind (mental quietness where wandering thoughts have departed due to your concentration) that you cultivate is why many visualization methods work, and it is hard to say that one in particular is better than all the others. However, it is indeed possible that some sets of instructions will incorporate more of the correct principles of cultivation practice or just happen to work better in producing results more effectively. In any case, this explains why different methods use different colors and numbers of petals for the channels, or recommend that you should just visualize chakras alone, or just channels, or both together. Once again, just as in practicing the martial arts to learn a specific skill, one should analyze things scientifically rather than get caught up in mystical ideas about the techniques.

When it is said that a set of particular tantric instructions like this are transmitted to students along lineages, you must remember to interpret everything in terms of fundamental principles rather than assuming that any secrets are being passed such as the true location, color or number of petals for a chakra, or that certain objects should absolutely be visualized in an inalterable particular way. You will never know the effectiveness of a visualization practice unless you practice it yourself, and its effectiveness will certainly vary according to individuals. The point of all such practices is to generally produce a quiet, focused state of mind through the method of focusing on images held internally at certain regions of the body, and whether they are really opening up the channels by diverting chi to those regions according to the assumed *modus operandi* is another matter entirely.

For this inner heat yoga tradition, one can even perform these visualizations in conjunction with breath retention techniques wherein one holds their breath. You have to be careful about such activities, however, because overly ardent practitioners can hurt themselves if they do this over strenuously, which is why the personal instructions handed down on how to practice correctly become important. Pranayama is not the only activity that can be combined with internal tantric visualizations. You can even perform these types of visualizations in conjunction with specific physical exercises for loosening the body, such as yoga *asanas* and martial arts positions, and they can be engaged in through rotation. Another particularly effective meditation, similar to the principles used in anapana practice, is to view the body as an empty shell within when doing these visualizations.

When engaging in this inner heat yoga technique, the typical practice is to meditate on all four chakras, visualizing them all at the same time. These are the instructions given in *"The Hevajra Root Tantra"* (Skt. *Hevajra mula tantra*), *"The Sambhuta Explanatory Tantra"* (Skt. *Samputa tantra raja tika*), and in other sources including the transmissions handed down from the ancient mahasiddhas including the famous Krishnacharya. More precisely, these instructions relate that you should focus on visualizing the four chakras, the three channels (left, right, and *sushumna*) and also a mantric syllable at each of the four chakras.

If we changed traditions, the letter used would change accordingly, for its only purpose is to serve as a focus of attention. In the Indian tradition, the mantric syllable would be in the form of a Sanskrit letter whereas it would be in the form of a Tibetan, Greek or Hebrew letter in those traditions accordingly. The letter just serves as an extra focus of attention, and in some traditions is replaced by a small flame or other figure.

For the explicit details on visualizing the chakras, let us turn to the highly recommended Tsong Khapa's "Six Yogas of Naropa" commentary itself, which relates the following instructions:

> Generally speaking, the practice for envisioning the mantric syllables at the chakras can be done either elaborately or else simply.
>
> In the former method, one visualizes a syllable at the center of each chakra, as well as on each of the petals. However, the oral instructions of this tradition do not elucidate this more elaborate process. Instead, they advocate that we should simply visualize a mantric syllable at the center of each of the four chakras. This is also the process taught in The *Sambhuta Explanatory Yantra* and in the wirings of many of the Indian mahasiddhas.
>
> Therefore solely to meditate on the *AH*-stroke mantric syllable at the navel chakra [as some teachers today recommend], or to meditate on the *AH*-stroke at the navel chakra together with *HAM* at the forehead chakra, is not sufficient. One should also bring in meditation on the syllables at the heart and throat chakras. This is important.

The manner of this meditation is as follows. One sits in the bodily posture described earlier. The place where the *AH*-stroke mantric syllable is to be visualized is the center of the central channel, just in front of the spinal column, at the place where the channel runs through the navel chakra. One should only meditate on the syllable as being at that point.

The process is as follows. One observes the navel chakra, known as "the wheel of emanation." At its center one envisions the *AH*-stroke syllable, standing upon a tiny moon cushion. It is in its Sanskrit form, which resembles the Tibetan character *shad* in the Tibetan classical script [i.e., the vertical stroke that divides Tibetan sentences]. It is red in color, and stands upright.

As for the syllable at the heart chakra, known as "the wheel of truth," which has eight petals, the place of this chakra is at the central channel just in front of the spine, at the point midway between the two nipples. One meditates only on the point at the center of the central channel. In this process of meditation one observes a tiny moon disk at the center of the chakra, and upon it a blue syllable *HUM*, its head pointing downward. One meditates that is has the power to cause the bodhimind substance to descend like falling snow.

Next one concentrates on the chakra known as "the wheel of enjoyment," which has sixteen petals. The place of this chakra is at the throat [i.e. behind the Adam's apple], and again the central channel runs through it, just in front of the spinal column. It is there that one place's one concentration, and observes a tiny moon disk, a tiny red syllable *OM* standing upright upon it.

Finally one focuses upon the chakra at the crown of the head, known as "the wheel of great ecstasy," which has thirty-two petals, the central channel running up the center of it. One observes a moon disk at its center, a white syllable *HAM* standing upon it, its head pointed downward.

With all four of these chakras it is important to remember that the central channel runs through the center of them, and the side channels wrap around and constrict the central channel at the places of the chakras. It is important to conduct the meditations at the level of the knots, and to envision each mantric syllable as being at the center of the central channel. ...

> Although most oral transmission [of this Six Yogas system] teach that one should meditate on the mantric syllables at the center of the chakras, in some it is not clearly taught that one should meditate only from within the center of the central channel. If this point is not emphasized and one meditates without doing so, the vital energies will not be drawn into the central channel. Consequently one will miss the essential purpose of the instruction.

> As for the size of the mantric syllables such as the syllable HUM [mentioned above in the quotation], it is a standard practice to visualize them as being the size of a mustard seed. However, the smaller that one can envision them, and the more clearly one can do so, the easier it becomes to draw the energies inside. [*Tsongkhapa's Six Yogas of Naropa*, Glenn H. Mullin (Snow Lion Publications, New York, 1996), pp. 139-164.]

You can find this basic method of cultivation, which involves visualizing four chakras along the length of the *sushumna*, used in a variety of different spiritual schools that focus on body energy cultivation, and is even illustrated in a western alchemy book by Michael Maiers, the *"Atalanta Fugiens"* (Emblem 17), which you can find on the internet. It is said that the Hopi Indians and Sufis even used this basic technique for some of their cultivation practices.

The even more basic idea of this visualization is to concentrate on visualizing the four main chakras of the body within you that run up the *sushumna* ... or a little flame, letter, seed or other tiny shining point of concentration at the center of those four chakras. The letter can be Hebrew, Tibetan, Greek, Sanskrit – it doesn't actually matter because all you want is just a provisional point of focus for the visualization practice. You try to visualize the point, flame, letter, etc. as shiny and bright.

One should only do such practices AFTER having spent some significant time with preliminary cultivation practices such as emptiness meditation, anapana, pranayama, and the white skeleton visualization. These practices will slowly open up many of the body's channels prior to this technique, whose usage all alone, without this prior opening of channels, can lead to energetic results which most people simply cannot handle.

You can also reduce the set of chakra points from four to three by concentrating on just the third eye chakra, heart chakra, and belly chakra. You can see pictures of these in "Tao and Longevity" by Nan Huai-chin. Some *nei-gong* schools in China take this approach and say you should recite the mantra "mmmm" at the region of the third eye, the mantra "ahhh" at the region of the heart, and the mantra "hunn" in the dantian, the belly chakra.

You are told to recite these mantras at those locations, and match the practice with your breath to draw the chi into your sushumna central channel. What most Chinese practitioners don't recognize is that this is also a Tibetan Buddhist practice, which is to recite the mantra "Ah Om Hung" [Om = Ohm = mmm, Hung = Hun = Hung = Hum = hunn, etc.] at the third eye, heart and belly chakra locations.

This is Samantabhadra's mantra technique for opening up the central channel. Practitioners of Tibetan esoteric yoga are told to do this for years, so this "secret Chinese *nei-gong* exercise" is basically the very well-known Samantabhadra mantric approach to helping open the central channel combined with the idea of the three Taoist elixir fields and three chakras of Buddhism that separate the Desire, Form and Formless cultivation realms. Once again, you can find this in "Tao and Longevity" and must recognize that it is basically the same thing.

These practices are usually kept secret in most traditions because people who do them, if they are young and keep a check on their virility through sexual restraint, can with concentration unleash all sorts of energy streams in their body. Those yang chi energy streams, also known as kundalini energies, will push through the body's chi channels to open them and clear them of obstructions. If that process is suddenly initiated with intensity all at once, rather than accomplished slowly over time, it will be extremely hot and painful. Once released, because channels open through, the force cannot be stopped but must be left alone to run its course. When it happened to me the period of intensity lasted for several months, and you must abandon yourself to the process and keep away from worldly activities as much as possible during that time so that you can continue to cultivate an empty mind, which helps its completion. Most people cannot bear these transformations engendered unless they have first cultivated their body for several years prior to this sort of practice, which martial arts, when combined with emptiness meditation, helps you accomplish. This is the level of real yang chi arising in the body, and few martial artists ever reach it.

You're supposed to have an empowerment to do such practices, and do lots of preparatory work prior to them, because that necessity gives teachers the chance to make sure the wrong people don't learn this material until they're mature enough and their bodies are ready to handle the painful consequences of all the channel openings suddenly happening. The correct sequence of the openings, and the various phenomena that arise when you cultivate correctly, are detailed in "The Little Book of Hercules" and "Tao and Longevity."

You need the right view on what's supposed to happen as to body changes and how you should cultivate your mind during such practices, otherwise you'll always be clinging to the physical body and thinking it's you as you cultivate this stage of transformation. If you cultivate such visualizations correctly along with the attendant exercises, all your chi energies will come up. You will get the gong-fu, as discussed, and all sorts of super powers and other abilities can arise. You can also release energy streams that your body is not ready to handle, so these materials are usually restricted to students who have been practicing for years, and thus have cleared their channels to some prior extent.

If you want to practice the white bone skeleton visualization, which is a lot safer, has no empowerment requirement and offers the martial arts benefits I mentioned, then all you really need to do is buy a little skeleton from some store like the **Anatomical Charts Company**, and memorize the bones so you can close your eyes and visualize the skeleton within your body as it lays. You always start the visualization with the left big toe, and you work from below upwards to the top of the body. You visualize the left toe bone, then the bones in your left foot, then the bones in your right foot, and then the bones in your left leg and so forth rising upwards. You look at your body and visualize the bones within it – the image being white rather than brown in color - and you hold that image with stability as you move upwards.

You can switch the order around to what's convenient to you in the upper areas of the torso, but you should always start the visualization at the feet, and in particular with the left big toe. After you visualize that your entire body is just a white skeleton sitting there, you imagine that the skeleton turns to dust, which blows away, and nothing is left but empty space. You try to forget your body and mind, and rest in an experience of empty mind that is similar to empty space.

With this simple technique you'll end up cultivating all the chi channels throughout your whole body in time and will not have to specifically focus on visualizing the *sushumna* or left and right channels, or the front and back channels either as taught in some Taoist practices. As mentioned, it doesn't happen instantly or right away. Everything takes time, especially when it comes to cultivating a mind of stability and the inner energies of your body.

This is harder to cultivate than just the *wai-gong* or external martial arts. But this is the path to becoming a great martial artist, one of those who receives the secret transmissions and become a lineage holder of a school or even skilled enough to become the founder of a new school or tradition. The white skeleton visualization, in conjunction with anapana and simple meditation practice of inner watching of thoughts, are all you really need to cultivate your internal energy to a high level. These alone will end up cultivating your chi and channels without any need of the esoteric techniques related.

I always tell people that if they're going to practice the white skeleton visualization, that they should also concentrate on their hands because a martial artist needs to use them, too. Don't just focus on the feet but also do the hand bones carefully including the palms and fingers, and the sacrum as well because it is also ultra important. The shoulder blades, ribs, pelvis and spine should also not be ignored. Most people will usually have some difficulty with the chi penetrating through the shoulders and also the buttocks, so don't ignore these regions.

There are so many scientific studies out there in the field of peak sports performance which will tell you, even for golf or for sports like lacrosse and so forth, that if you practice visualizing a particular movement that you want to perfect, the visualization will help you achieve it quicker and to a higher skill level than what you normally can achieve just by practicing that movement alone. You can master it quicker and to a higher degree of excellence by using visualization.

Thus, Arnold Schwarzenegger used visualization while weight lifting to help build his muscles and perfect his routines. Many, many people have used visualization in their quest for superior sports performance, and you constantly hear this from great athletes. If you're stuck on trying to perfect a martial arts form and you really can't get the movements right, you should sit down and visualize somebody who is correctly doing what you are trying to master in movement. You visualize yourself doing the movement from within the body looking outwards, and also as a third person watching yourself execute it correctly, or you can just keep tracing the other person's perfect movements in your mind. And believe it or not, you'll get really good at it that way – it will help you transform your martial arts practice incredibly so. In short, mental rehearsal will definitely improve your skill level. It will definitely enhance your athletic performance. That's a little trick that they never tell you, but it's extremely useful.

There are lots of various applications of visualization practices, and many types of visualization exercise. For instance, we know a very traditional Ba Gua Zhang teacher who always recommends two visualization practices. The first visualization practice is for being able to actually use the body weapons you're training in, for example, a specific type of punch or palm strike. The visualization method is for you to pick a target spot you want to master hitting, and you always visualize going after it. For months at a time, for every person you see – whether you meet them or see them walking towards you on the street - you visualize hitting that target spot on their body. As your body fills with chi and you match this with the visualization, you sort of build that into your nervous system. The mind doesn't know any difference between the visualization of whether you did it from the event of actually physically doing it. So in practicing this way with visualization, it is as if you actually did it, and thus your practice improves.

This is not a visualization for meditation progress, but for learning how to do a skill correctly or with more power. The results, in terms of cultivating internal energy, are far less then learning how to hold a topic steady within your mind, as in the skeleton visualization. Nevertheless you need to know about the different ways to improve your martial arts technique.

The other method that he taught was that even if you're sitting on an airplane somewhere, you can sit there and you should be going through your technique in your head using your imagination. You'll know you're doing it right because your body will start to want to move with the technique. You might start to even jerk a little bit just doing the visualization techniques over and over again. For whatever reason, because there are different theories on the matter, mental training improves motor skills, so I highly recommend incorporating it along with physical practice as it will elevate your martial arts skills and performance level. Even if you don't cultivate your internal energies, I want you to have new dimensions of training which you can pick up from this book.

I can tell you many, many stories about hockey teams, golfers and others who did visualization practices, and excelled because of that practice. There are studies where they would take basketball players and put them into three groups: those who just practiced shooting hoops four hours a day versus those who did visualizations for one of those four hours. The group which did the visualizations always scored better. In field hockey, those who used relaxation with visualization practice improved their goal shooting by 160% versus 70% for those who just did the physical practices.

In Olympic golf training, one group visualized their ball going into the hole all the time, and their results showed a 30% putting improvement. Another group visualized their ball going away from the cup, and their results dropped by 21%. A third group, which just did regular physical practice, only improved their results by 11%.

In another Olympic training study performed by Russians, one group of athletes engaged in only physical exercises, or physical training. A second group spent 75% of their time in physical training, and 25% in mental training. A third group spent 50% of their time in physical training and 50% in mental training, and a fourth group did 25% physical training and 75% mental training. Those who spent 75% of their time on mental training improved the most and performed the best.

Because the neural pathways you build in the brain tend to follow the mind, through visualization practice you're basically creating circuits in your body, neural pathways that your body is going to end up using. Therefore if you model your movements on a martial artist like Jet Li and you continue to play those images over and over and over again in your mind from having viewed a movie or whatever, that's going to start to be imprinted in your mind, and it will become easier to actually physically develop that skill in the same flow style as Jet Li. Your movements will actually start to become like anyone you model through visualization practice, so pick your models well.

The idea is to visualize specific behaviors over and over again to help train muscle memory because the mental images can act as a prelude to muscular performance. Do it slow at first, and then faster later. Warning: Never repeat a wrong image hundreds or thousands of times, or you will just be ingraining the wrong habit.

You must know the optimum results you want, visualize those results, and work towards them in your practice routines. What you visualize should represent a perfected state of achievement – perfection in form and flow. This might be your footwork, or arm movements, or how you twist or turn and so on.

Visualization practice ties in with the principles of "**deep practice**," which we'll also discuss, and you should link these two ideas together. In short, no one teaches you this but you can use this mechanism of visualization in mastering the martial arts. It will definitely speed up your progress. It's a type of mental training that can be used during your off hours or even during the course of rehabilitation from some hurt or injury.

Today in science we talk about the mind-body phenomena, but scientists don't recognize that mind-body phenomena means consciousness and chi. The chi of your body - your body energies, your life force - and consciousness (your thoughts or your mind) are linked. That's the basic unstated principle. They represent a coin with two sides.

Wherever you put your mind in your body, your chi is going to go to that point or region. If you think of a point outside of your body, it will go there, too. If you think of your left thigh bone right now and you visualize it, all your chi is going to go there. If after learning how to visualize all of the bones of your body, you then combine that anatomical knowledge with the practice of the white skeleton visualization to hold that image with stability, all of your chi will flow to all those bones ... and the chi channels along those lengths will start to open simply because chi is rushing there. And you will be learning concentration practice which, when released, leads to an empty mind and the subsequent activation of chi energies due to that internal mental quiet.

Actually, any steady visualization that produces a quiet mind causes all your chi to arise (we should say "the state of mental quiet causes your chi to arise"), and that's why this practice is so effective at transforming your chi channels and getting your chi to move. The fact that chi runs to a region is a related method of healing, but not an explanation for the true power behind this technique. In any case, with one visualization you therefore end up cultivating all the important chi channels and meridians throughout your body. What martial artist could object to that, especially because you are learning anatomy at the same time?

Not only does the state of empty mind lead to the arising of chi, but that chi, in opening up your internal channels and with the concentration of the bone visualizations, will even help to transform your bones. This is hard to do since they represent the densest earth element of your body, but this cultivation or meditation or visualization practice – however you want to call it - will actually help open up all of the chi channels along those bones, which is basically the entire extent of the body. It is the one-pointedness that does this rather than the image of the skeleton, but that image gives guidance for concentration to have some form to focus on that just happens to match the routes of your chi channels. That helps some, too, but is not the major determinant of the progress in opening your channels.

The progress comes from concentration. Visualizing an apple with stability would also end up opening your chi channels if you could actually do it. However, there are multiple benefits to specifically visualizing your internal skeleton for both martial arts progress and other reasons that we cannot go into. In any case, visual image concentration practice is really incredible for cultivating the yang chi of the body. So much energy comes up that this practice tends to stir up sexual desire, too, and we'll soon discuss that as well.

When sexual desire is stirred up as the result of some exercise, it is starting to touch on the outskirts of yang chi cultivation. If you make very good progress in your inner martial arts practice, there will come a time when sexual desires, anger, depression, irritation, fierce violent tendencies, jumpiness, short temperedness, edginess, hatreds and mood swings will all tend to arise as your raw (not refined) yang chi finally starts arising in the body.

Bruce Frantzis once wrote that Fukien White Crane masters, and any martial artists who employed visualization and self-hypnosis practices, would especially encounter these problems. This is because in using meditation cultivation techniques, their true yang chi would finally arise, and its initial arising is provoking in nature since the chi flow is always encountering obstructions. This is explained in the Fourth Labor of Hercules, which represents this raw chi as a fierce boar or wild half human, half animal centaur. Hercules was only able to finally conquer the fierce boar in his Labors by chasing it into a snowdrift, and the whiteness of that snow represents the cultivation of a pure mind or empty mind which you can achieve through meditation. My teacher would give me liver medicines at this stage, such as **Lung Tan Xie Gan** pill and ox bile capsules, but whatever you use to help clear liver heat and fire should depend on your own personal situation.

These problems of irritation, annoyance, angry outbursts and violent tendencies will especially be the case as your liver meridian starts to clear due to these rising raw yang energies, and this is often a troublesome issue until the channels finally clear of obstruction and your chi tends to purify because you no longer hold to it. During this time it is recommended to undergo detoxification routines for the liver, such as ingesting liver drainage formulas, to help limit the problem. But in essence, the quickest way of getting rid of the problem is to reach a higher stage of emptiness meditation by letting go, in which case the chi channel obstructions will open and your chi will purify further.

Pranayama practice basically involves trying to hold your breath, which in turn tries to force open chi channels. Anapana is basically letting go of the body while keeping conscious of your breathing. Eventually your mind quiets, your breath quiets, the two become one, and your real chi arises within you during that subsequent state of emptiness, or mental calming.

As to visualization practice, it works on an entirely different modus operandi of just trying to hold a stable visual image from the start, and then releasing your state of mental stability to experience a quiet mind free of wandering thoughts. For *nei-gong*, rather than martial arts performance, visualization practice requires that you focus on creating a stationary, stable visual image within your mind. If that involves a point or location within your body, then your chi goes there and that also helps to open up a particular area of the body as a side benefit.

There is a whole field of meditations, called "kasina meditations," that are concentration practices which martial artists or anyone can use to learn how to stabilize their minds. They are also a form of training for one-pointedness, which is the ability to concentrate and hold to a thought for a long period of time without wavering. They are called absorptions because absorption is another name for the fact that your mind remains with a topic, another term being concentration. Basically, these are concentration practices using different objects as the focus of attention.

The white skeleton visualization practice, called the body impurity practice in Buddhist terms, is one of these kasina absorption or concentration practices. It just happens to simultaneously help cultivate your physical body to a better degree than other types of absorptions, or concentration exercises.

You can find many other kasina practices in the book called "The Path of Purification" ("Visuddhimagga," by Buddhaghosa) which gives people a number of concentrations, some of which are visualizations wherein you have to hold a purely visual image in your mind with steadiness and without being distracted.

The kasina meditations are simply different objects used as the focus of concentration, and concentration by itself will not produce any special result except the ability to calm your mind of wandering thoughts. Once your chi channels open, and you go past the stage of cultivating chi and *shen* to achieve true samadhi, then by using your mind you can produce what we call miracles, or miraculous results. If you just practice concentration, and can hold a thought with stability, you just attain a steady mind but cannot produce these miraculous results until you penetrate through to the root source of both mind and matter, and that's why you become able to perform miracles. When you achieve true dhyana or samadhi, you can demonstrate them.

What are some examples?

As I explained in "How to Measure and Deepen Your Spiritual Realization," also known as "Measuring Meditation," at a high enough stage of attainment someone can cultivate a certain mastery of the earth element. If they attain the corresponding earth element samadhi, which means being able to create or manipulate the earth element using consciousness, they can, as just one of the resultant skills, be able to achieve the superpower of standing in the sky by having the earth element appear wherever they want, namely underneath their feet. Mastering the earth element samadhi will also enable them to make visible (non-living) replicas of themselves.

In short, the kasina meditations lead to one-pointed concentration skills, and with the attainment of samadhi through the road of mastering one-pointed concentration, you can then learn how matter and mind are ultimately connected. Then you can learn how to manipulate consciousness-stuff on your own, and thereby how to master the various material elements since they are, in their ultimate nature, just consciousness. Some masters will choose to develop specific skills in manipulating consciousness, which are what we call superpowers, and others will not. It's like choosing to learn a specific type of martial arts, or choosing not to do so. Everyone has a physical body, but few choose to learn martial arts and of those who do, there are endless things you can possibly learn, all of which require practice. If you don't choose to learn how to practice new forms and movements, then you can't do those special forms of martial arts, like *Dim Mak*.

The stories of miraculous powers linked to elemental kasinas are just examples of what you can master if you penetrate through to the root source of mind to become able to master matter, since it is essentially consciousness, and then learn how to master the manifestation of a specific element in particular. The ability to master an element (fire, water, earth, air, space) does not necessarily arise from the specific kasina, such as by concentrating on the color yellow to be able to produce gold. That is a misunderstanding. No one knows how it works until you attain that samadhi attainment, and those attainments seem common among masters of many traditions. All we can say, since we cannot yet manipulate matter with our own minds, is that we will understand how it is actually accomplished when we personally attain the Tao. The idea of concentrating on the color blue, yellow, red and so forth is a spur to get you to do concentration practice of a certain sort, and can certainly lead to higher attainments and the mastery of the physical elements if through this route you develop concentration and then attaint he Tao, but as to how the transformations actually work is only known to masters who get that far. Even so, these capabilities of mastering the elements are indeed possible if you cultivate the Tao.

It is said that someone who masters the water samadhi attainment (called a samadhi or absorption since it means being able to manipulate that particular element) can develop the ability to manifest rivers and lakes, make the earth or buildings quake, and have water appear wherever they want. Mastering the fire element samadhi can be the basis for such powers as being able to burn other objects at will, burning one's body at the time of death, countering fire with fire, and so on. The wind element samadhi accomplishment is the basis for being able to walk with the speed of wind and causing windstorms. Mastering the space samadhi accomplishment enables an individual to walk through walls and earth, create space inside rocks and mountains, or see hidden objects.

There are other samadhis such as the light, red, blue, white and yellow kasina accomplishments. For instance, the yellow samadhi is said to be the basis for being able to create yellow forms, or having something turn into gold. Is that how it really works? It may not be so. However, you certainly do need to learn how to develop concentration (so your mind settles, channels open, yang chi arises, etc.) to progress in attaining the Tao, whereby such accomplishments become possible. Whether they actually involve visualizing colors or manipulating the consciousness in some other mechanism is unknown to us. Nevertheless, the stories from countless traditions of these capabilities assures us that they are possible.

You can transform a rock into gold because the rock is essentially consciousness and gold is consciousness, too, and however the mechanism works, you simply learn how to manipulate consciousness so that it changes from one form into another. It is not something out of nothing, but transforming one type of consciousness-stuff into another type of consciousness-stuff. You learn how to turn one type of consciousness into another. You learn how to perform a transformation. Due to samadhi or Tao attainments, your mind has already reached the root of consciousness, and so you learn how to use it to perform various functions, or manipulations that we are calling "transformations."

Obviously this cannot be done at the level of simple human thought, such as the types of thought used in trying to solve a math problem, or the self-talk thoughts running around in your head as you go about your daily work or interact with people. Who can think of an apple and have it appear? Who can, just by thinking, be able to walk through a wall unimpeded? It has to do with penetrating through to the roots of consciousness, to discovering what pure consciousness is, and discovering that phenomena are actually that pure consciousness, too. Then you have to learn how to manipulate consciousness in a certain way to get the particular effect you want, and your own body has to develop high enough gong-fu to achieve this.

If a master stops at the level of realizing there is no self, but does not penetrate through to realizing that there are no genuine self-so phenomena either (because they are essentially consciousness or mind), their capabilities along these lines remain limited. One has to reach the level of recognizing that inherent emptiness and interdependent origination (the cause and effect world of matter and consciousness) are one, and become able to manipulate this. Only a great fully enlightened Buddha, who resolves things to the absolute root, knows how to do all these things, but to do them still takes practice for mastery. As stated, your internal chi and channel gong-fu has to be high enough, too, when any of these abilities depend upon the body.

Mastering a kasina actually means mastering concentration on a specific form. Mastering the accompanying superpower (which is what mastering a kasina actually means rather than just the idea of mastering a certain type of mental concentration using a particular object) means you mastered a particular samadhi attainment, which may or may not be based on the accompanying kasina. Such attainments are past the level of *shen* cultivation. They involve getting to the root stuff of what pure consciousness or awareness is itself, and learning how to manipulate this.

Some people call this the *nirmanakaya* capability of Buddhism, which actually means the ability to transform or manipulate all forms of consciousness. A single thought is a *nirmanakaya*, since it is a projection, transformation or manifestation of consciousness. Any transformations of consciousness are also actually *nirmanakaya* manifestations or "transformation bodies." It doesn't just mean a projection of something in consciousness for others to see, hear and so on. The ability to transform one type of matter into another, as represented in kasina miracles, is actually a type of transformation, and thus a *nirmanakaya* performance.

The *nirmanakaya* capability is typically considered the ability to be reborn or simply project oneself, or image of oneself, in other realms at will, such as letting others see a body double of oneself. This, too, is a type of samadhi accomplishment due to a special type of concentration or use of the mind, but is only accomplished at the level of Tao cultivation. It is not exactly the same as the earth element kasina/samadhi accomplishment where you can make copies or images of oneself, but is actually a physical presence projected of oneself in another realm of consciousness. It is not something that arises out of the human body either, such as is deemed happens with astral projection.

This body double *nirmanakaya* capability (sometimes called the *yang shen* attainment of Taoism when limited to the earth sphere) has also been reported of some great martial arts masters, but it is really only those who attain the Tao and strive to cultivate these abilities who can do them, and it is not that a martial arts master attained them because he was a martial artist. Furthermore, if you don't cultivate these types of capabilities then you won't have them even though you have the capability of doing them by virtue of the fact that you attain the Tao. This is why some Arhats have superpowers and others do not. It is all a matter of the choosing to cultivate these abilities to help others, or simply remaining satisfied with the accomplishment of self-liberation without the need to cultivate anything further. After liberation, some believe the task is done, so there is no need to learn how to cultivate anything else, such as these capabilities. Great Buddhas and Bodhisattvas, however, vow to learn everything because further capabilities open up more ways to help people.

These abilities can help you teach or liberate the others in the realm of samsara, so that is why some enlightened masters cultivate them. They don't cultivate them because they are "cool" to have, for at that level you don't need anything or really want anything for yourself (there is no self to enjoy them). Since they are possibilities of your true mind, functions which you can master because they are consciousness, why not learn to master them? The whole universe is you and can be explored. Everything is consciousness and you yourself are a functioning of consciousness that can manipulate them. Because they can be used for the greater good of compassionate service to help others awaken (they are never used for selfish means such as making money, knowing the future for one's entertainment or personal advantage, for what self is there who would receive such advantage – do), some realized ones therefore choose to cultivate them.

Let us summarize some of these kasina or samadhi attainments, though there are countless more. These are only some of the easier ones masters choose to cultivate, and are used as an example to help you understand the process and resultant capabilities. The "Visuddhimagga" states,

> Of these, the earth kasina is the basis for such powers as the state described as "Having been one, he becomes many", etc., and stepping or standing or sitting on space or on water by creating earth, and the acquisition of the bases of mastery by the limited and measureless method.

The water kasina is the basis for such powers as diving in and out of the earth, causing rain, storms, creating rivers and seas, making the earth and rocks and palaces quake. The fire kasina is the basis for such powers as smoking, flaming, causing showers of sparks, countering fire with fire, ability to burn only what one wants to burn, causing light for the purpose of seeing visible objects with the divine eye, burning up the body by means of the fire element at the time of attaining Nirvana.

The air kasina is the basis for such powers as going with the speed of the wind, causing wind storms.

The blue kasina is the basis for such powers as creating black forms, causing darkness, acquisition of the bases of mastery by the method of fairness and ugliness, and attainment of the liberation by the beautiful.

The yellow kasina is the basis for such powers as creating yellow forms, resolving that something shall be gold, acquisition of the bases of mastery in the way stated, and attainment of the liberation by the beautiful.

The red kasina is the basis for such powers as creating red forms, acquisition of the bases of mastery in the way stated, and attainment of the liberation by the beautiful.

The white kasina is the basis for such powers as creating white forms, banishing stiffness and torpor, dispelling darkness, causing light for the purpose of seeing visible objects with the divine eye.

The light kasina is the basis for such powers as creating luminous forms, banishing stiffness and torpor, dispelling darkness, causing light for the purpose of seeing visible objects with the divine eye.

The space kasina is the basis for such powers as revealing the hidden, maintaining postures inside the earth and rocks by creating space inside them, travelling unobstructed through walls, and so on.

The classification "above, below, around, exclusive, measureless" applies to all kasinas; for this is said: "He perceives the earth kasina above, below, around, exclusive, measureless", and so on.

... Measureless means measureless intentness. He is intent upon the entirety with his mind, taking no measurements in this way: "This is its beginning, this is its middle." [*Visuddhimagga: The Path of Purification,*

95

trans. by Bhikkhu Nanamoli, (Buddhist Publication Society, Sri Lanka, 2011), pp. 166-167.]

These super powers are often the very same ones you read about in martial artist novels, and which you see in the Hong Kong, Taiwanese and Chinese gong-fu movies, like being able to fly in space, or sit in space, and dive into the Earth, and run with the speed of the wind.

"The Path of Purification" section on the kasina meditations actually tells you what mental absorptions at the level of the Tao you must cultivate to be able to accomplish certain extraordinary supernormal powers that transform the basis of consciousness into phenomena. But it won't work for you unless you have some degree of genuine samadhi. And you cannot attain samadhi or the Tao unless you have already laid the necessary preliminary foundation in *nei-gong* and gone on to start cultivating *Tao-gong*. That's the secret no one tells you! But, in using these kasina meditations as the focus of practice, you can attain a quiet, empty mind (this is called attaining concentration), open up your chi channels, lay the foundation for higher practices, and move on from there. But don't think that just by visualizing the yellow element all day that you will become able to transform everything into gold.

You must realize that the stuff of consciousness is you, is everywhere, and there is no inside it or outside of it. This is why the "Visuddhimagga" says the mental state is measureless, everywhere, wherein there is no in or out, beginning or ending, up or down. This is dealing with mind-stuff, so it is a stage of realization rather than imagination (though of course we can say that everything is imagination or unreal when compared to the truest sense of the absolute nature itself). It is saying that you must reach the stage where the mind becomes boundless, infinite, empty. This is the stage past *shen* cultivation when the mind expands to encompass all. You discover the existence of *shen* at the same time that your mind empties of thoughts, and your mental horizons start to become emptier, wider, vaster, limitless. Hence, one simply takes the path of producing a quiet mind by concentrating on a particular kasina topic, and when one achieves this emptiness samadhi they can eventually progress further to the stage where they develop powers over an element via further cultivation.

Once again, these various superpower capabilities are real. They are possible and stories of their existence have been passed down to us from countless spiritual schools and traditions, usually signifying that someone has reached a certain stage of attainment. They don't signify enlightenment, but just a high stage of attainment of the ability to manipulate consciousness from one form into another, and we consider one of those forms "matter" when it is actually consciousness-stuff. They are consciousness absorptions you cultivate with your mind to learn how to manipulate the stuff of consciousness itself into physical forms or physical effects in the physical world, which is itself consciousness. Thus, you can attain this on the route of martial arts excellence, but only if you devote yourself to cultivating your mind and the road of cultivating the Tao.

This is the possibility of kasina meditation, and there are many more types of manifestation possible beyond these introductory few because the possible functions of the mind are myriad, uncountable, and all sorts of phenomena, and non-phenomenal things, can be produced if one learns how to penetrate through to the source. That requires a purification of consciousness and commitment to cultivation efforts to even get this far.

If you don't open up the macrocosmic circulation, you won't have a foundation for these higher attainments, so desiring them is useless. It is cultivation that enables you to attain any capability, whether at the level of mundane martial arts or the level of manipulating the stuff of consciousness itself once enlightened. To be able to create and then hold a mental image in your mind is actually one of the myriad functions of consciousness, so you can see how learning how to do this at a junior level prepares you, as in training your muscles, for being able to do it at a more profound, foundational level that is represented by the kasina accomplishments. These are all absorptions or concentrations you can practice after you have resolved your mind to its deepest depths, and then you know how to manipulate consciousness to get these special effects. As stated, the number of things you can do is endless because it is all mind, and you resolve the mystery of the mind by penetrating through to the root via the road of meditation practice that should always accompany martial arts efforts.

You won't get those results unless, like I said previously, until well past the stage where you open up the central channel, and then the microcosmic circulation (the River Chariot rotation), and then the full macrocosmic circulation. That's the most minor set of requirements for laying the foundation for these sorts of achievements, though it requires more *nei-gong* progress than even that! Nevertheless, you now know the start and how it's done.

Once you achieve sufficient *nei-gong* and move on to formless samadhi attainments, then you can get the martial arts super powers. If you don't open up the central channel and the River Chariot rotation, however, it's never going to happen. It doesn't mean that it's not good practice for you, it's just never going to happen. You have to lay the foundation and from that start cultivating samadhi attainments.

The two techniques of anapana and the white skeleton visualization, by the way, are really two treasures, and secrets, of Chinese culture. They account for part of the reason why Buddhism was able to enter China without being barred by the government. It was because people cultivated those two methods and they actually transformed their bodies so much and achieved samadhi attainments that all of a sudden all of these abilities came out. And that's why people started accepting Buddhism so easily.

China at that time had Confucianism and it had Taoism, and Buddhism was a foreign import. The intelligencia of the time responded to its entry into the country, "Well, we don't need this foreign import coming in. It's not home grown." However, the regular people took these two practices just by themselves, they'd practice them religiously, and they would get the results that were promised in Buddhist sutras. There were countless cases where people attained. When that happens, what can you say? It's all fake? It doesn't work? It's all nonsense? No one could say anything against the claims of Buddhism, and so it was finally accepted into the nation.

The problem today is that people don't cultivate. It's not that they don't cultivate anapana and the white skeleton visualization, but they don't even cultivate the simple meditation of watching their thoughts! Another of the problems, even if you do practice, is that sometimes progress comes down to a matter of celibacy.

Now I don't want you to think that ultimate success in the high martial arts, or for the spiritual path, is ultimately a matter of celibacy, because that's a mistake and not what I said. People always get confused about this and misinterpret things, interjecting their own opinions and biases. You don't have to be celibate to succeed. You just have to refrain from losing your energies carelessly and in abundance so that they can be used to open your chi channels. Masturbation is the worst affront along these lines of energy loss.

A lot of martial artists read these old classics, especially in Taoism, and they don't understand this emphasis on celibacy called "not losing the elixir" or "not leaking *jing*." In India, this idea of retaining the semen is called *brahmacharya*. What it basically means is the following ...

If you're a martial artist and you start upon the road of meditation and pranayama and you don't really feel any internal energies, it's probably because you haven't sat long enough or your mind is probably not empty enough. If your mind is empty, that's a state of yin. Yang will definitely arise when you cultivate yin, or mental emptiness, so your yang chi energies will rise if you do this correctly and sufficiently and long enough. That yang chi will work to open up your chi channels, and you'll pass through the stage of *qi-gong* to *nei-gong* quickly. If you lose that yang energy through any type of loss, it will not be available to open up your chi channels and help smoothen your chi circulation.

If you're young and you're full of vitality and you're not leaking your elixir with excessive masturbation or ejaculation within intercourse, those chi energy forces will be very strong and pronounced, and your channels can thus open quickly when those energies are allowed to work on that purpose. If you practice pranayama exercises then this, too, will tend to force your kundalini or yang chi to arise, especially if you have not been losing your energies. You'll often get an stronger effect if you've been retaining your generative energies and have been meditating, which helps them transform into chi, which in turn, in conjunction with an empty mind, will help open your chi channel meridians.

Your celibacy produces a latent power that is ready to arise, so there's a dragon there that can awaken and be used to your benefit. But if you're not accumulating and storing this energy (by avoiding ejaculation), there's no dragon there. It's like a fire hydrant which doesn't have any water pressure inside it, and therefore no water can flow through the outlet when it's opened. That's how celibacy helps you cultivate the stages of *qi-gong* and *nei-gong*. It is simply a matter of preventing energy loss so that more energies can be devoted to attaining the desired results of your practice.

4

THE ROLE OF SEX IN CHI DEVELOPMENT:
CELIBACY AND SEX ON THE PATH OF INNER GONG-FU

In my book "Twenty-Five Doors to Meditation," I go over twenty-five different meditations that people can cultivate, including the topic of Taoist sexual practice wherein you learn not to lose your energies during sexual relations. Because it's so important, I also wrote a special section on sexual discipline and the diet within "The Little Book of Meditation." This is important on the martial arts path, and actually is another form of martial arts, but between couples.

As to celibacy, or storing your sexual energies, celibacy is like storing water in a boiler wherein the water can evaporate to be steam in the pipes that can run through and open up the chi channels. It's only if you open up the chi channels, which means opening up your chakras and purifying your chi, and going through all of these body transformations of the *qi-gong* and *nei-gong* stages, that's when you can start to get a lot of the supernatural miraculous powers that you read about in some of these books.

They're not fictional achievements at all. It's just that most people never cultivate to the necessary stages of attainment. Part of that cultivation is marshalling your sexual energies so that they can, via a sort of pressure, produce a force that can open up your chi channels. Failing at this, you cannot get to real *nei-gong*, and thus these abilities are out of reach.

A lot of young men in their teens and twenties have so much vitality that it doesn't really matter whether they're celibate or not, even though masturbation and excessive ejaculation during intercourse definitely harms them. In terms of energy loss, masturbation is the worst of the two by far and should be eliminated from your life if at all possible. Traditional Chinese medicine and Ayurveda both state that many problems, both mental and physical, arise due to excessive masturbation by men. Perhaps while not young, but when you're older, you start to be able to definitely feel the loss of internal chi, energy and power when you ejaculate and lose your semen. That's how people arrived at these principles since the robustness of youth sometimes masks one's ability to notice changes in internal energy.

In any case, Taoism teaches men who have a sexual partner how to have sex without leaking because it's not a matter of strict celibacy, but it's a matter of no leakage, of not losing energy. Of course at the highest levels it is also about no-thought, and therefore not letting your mind be disturbed by thoughts of sex either. There are a lot of different approaches to this and you can read in some martial arts novels where the hero actually takes a consort to help him get over sexual desire or as a partner where the two can practice together. On the other hand, sometimes the novel will say that a man lost his powers and abilities because of sex, like Sampson in the Bible, which represents this idea perfectly.

Some books will give you a story line of, "Oh, well. The wife taught him how to do tantric sex where he didn't lose his power and he ended up making more progress." This is because the woman was also a cultivator with an excellent stage of chi channel purification, and the two were able to use sexual cultivation as an adjunct, and sometimes alternative, to anapana for opening up channel obstructions and cultivating internal energy. But who can find such a skilled partner with excellent chi and channels who is qualified for such practice – no one! So the topic of sex is a confusing issue for most people.

This is what people don't understand. For most people, sexual discipline is strictly a matter of 100% celibacy, but actually it's more than that – you should not even stir your mind with sexual desires and lose your energies carelessly in any way. On the other hand, you can still have sex if you just learn how not to lose the energies through ejaculation, and yet without restraining them or trying to stop their outward flow by pressing on acupuncture points if ejaculation has started. That popular technique will actually screw up a man's prostate and bladder. Women don't even need to worry about orgasm because a woman's body is designed differently, and the loss of energy through orgasm doesn't hurt her as much as a man, so the injunction of no orgasm does not hold.

A lot of martial artists have yet to learn about this topic because it's only in the last twenty years that the information has finally become available - through Taoism, martial arts, yoga, TCM and the like - that celibacy is a real boon to your spiritual practice. Prior to this, people didn't even realize that losing too much semen could cause eye floaters, headaches, dizziness, feelings of listlessness, weak muscles, knee problems, lower back pain, and so on.

Many cases of mental instability and depression are also linked to an excessive loss of semen, usually from masturbation more than intercourse. As you can get older you can feel the effects of this loss inside your body and know it to be true, but the western world is all about the enjoyment of sex so says very little about this. Western doctors would never ban a drug like Viagra, which makes sex possible for men during the years they should be treasuring their *jing*, even though it has been responsible for hundreds of cases of blindness and even death.

Once again, to make this concept clear I want you to remember the image of these old houses where they have radiators. The old radiators are giant metal heaters standing against the walls that heat old homes in wintertime. These old radiators start knocking furiously when the steam goes through them. They go, "Tink, tink, tink, tink!" and shake furiously because there is a boiler down below sending this steam through the pipes. It hits all these obstructions and so the pipes shake and rattle. If there's no water in the boiler, however, you can't get any steam in the pipes to heat the house.

With that in mind, if you're losing your *jing*, semen, generative forces, elixir, treasure or however you wish to call it, it's the same thing as emptying all of the water out of the boiler. Your chi channels won't be able to open because there will be no force available to push through the obstructions. *Jing* transforms into chi within your body, and without any *jing* you won't have any chi available to open up your chi routes.

In short, you must practice celibacy now and then to accumulate your energies, or simply learn how to have sex without leakage. Sex, it is said, often destroys the health of young men when they lose energy to the point of dissipation. Some queens or concubines in China, when the son of a contender was due to become the next Emperor, would try to kill him by sending him pretty maidens as a gift. They knew that he might not be able to control his sexual desires and might not have learned correct sexual technique we're discussing, and thus they hoped he might become weak and die from sexual dissipation through excessive loss. Talk about strategy! If it didn't work the unknowing young prince would still thank the Queen mightily and think highly of her forever for the gift!

My own teacher told me a story that when he went to military school, he had two special martial arts instructors who had both sworn off women and attributed their skills to this fact. One of these martial arts teachers had a big, fat belly. One day after all the students were gone and the room was empty, this teacher called him over and said, "Nan Huai Chin, I want you to punch me in the belly."

My teacher said, "No, Sifu. I can't. I can't. I dare not." He said, "Punch me in the stomach." "No, I can't." "Punch me in the stomach, it's an order!" So he said, "All right."

My teacher started to punch him in the stomach, and the teacher lifted him up when the punch connected with his flesh, and my teacher was sent flying across the room. And his teacher said afterwards, "I used to be sick all the time until I stopped losing my energy though sex. That capability comes from not fooling around with women."

If you can conserve your energies and transmute them, and you train, then you can learn lots of special skills according to how you train. But most people never train sufficiently and most people never conserve their energies. Nevertheless, this is the principle for being able to get to those high stages in martial arts. It doesn't mean you never have sex, but that you don't lose your energies carelessly, too frequently, or in volume. You can go read the Yellow Emperor's conversation in the "Plain Girl Sutra" to understand this.

Remember that there's a flip side to this too. Celibacy is not everything. If you just cultivate celibacy but you don't cultivate the opening of the chi channels by cultivating mental emptiness and you don't train with martial arts, you'll just get healthy from conserving your semen, and that's about all. It doesn't guarantee a long life if you cannot transmute it from cultivating emptiness meditation so that *jing* transforms into chi.

Some men who are old try to regain their lost vitality through stimulant formulations, but they never work and just cause the problem of excitation. Taoism and TCM suggest they eat sesame seeds, so you can find sesame milk in Korean stores that some people drink. In India, they say that pistachios will help men store their lost *jing*. Some people say lamb bone marrow will help restore it, too. The herbal formula **Liu Wei Di Huang Wan** helps some men because it's designed to replenish sexual energies and help the kidneys.

Actually, the best way is to practice emptiness meditation for awhile, and then your *jing* will tend to become restored, but most people don't know this simple practice and search for all sorts of stimulants in hopes it will help them become renewed. The big secret is that silent inner witnessing meditation, that opens up the chi channels, is the one thing that brings about *jing* and chi renewal. That's another reason to embark upon the path of *nei-gong*, because as you get older you will find the benefits quite worthwhile just for the mundane concerns of sickness, health and longevity that strike someone who is aging.

When you are making a soup, you have to know what ingredients you want in it if you have an idea what you want it to taste like. So for martial arts, you can design your own practice schedule if you know what you are trying to achieve. The most important thing for you to understand from this small book are the principles for attaining certain higher stages of gong-fu, and how to train for that.

Part of the road to the necessary foundational *nei-gong* is marshalling your sexual energies to some degree, and not losing them carelessly. It is a matter of not losing energies, and this is a bigger problem for men than for women. If you lose your energies they will not be there for opening up your chi channels. However, if you just hold those energies through forceful restraint without cultivating mental emptiness so that the transformation of *jing* into chi becomes possible, that's not exactly correct either.

After you get the Tao, of course, you can recover quickly if you ever lose your semen, so the focus is on getting there and how to do so. What you do after you achieve it is all up to you.

5
THE MYTHICAL MARTIAL ARTS – ARE THEY REALLY POSSIBLE?

One of the things we can now discuss are some of the super powers and super normal powers that you normally hear about when it comes to legends in martial arts. You can actually achieve these special abilities – it's not science fiction – after you first reach the level of *nei-gong* and then keep cultivating.

These are such powers as where you see swordsmen who can fly through the air and things like that. There are lots of stories of people who cultivated their internal energies to a level where they could do such things, and the individuals are almost always connected to spiritual traditions because these capabilities require you to cross over from purely physical chi cultivation to the cultivation of the metaphysical, which is the pursuit of the Tao.

The famous Tibetan Milarepa, for instance, could fly through the air. You can read of his story in "The Life of Milarepa" by Lobsang Lhalungpa. He had all sorts of unusual abilities he cultivated from his internal energies, such as being able to project body doubles and so forth.

The monk Chi Kung in China, who was also an Arhat, demonstrated many miraculous super powers as well, and if he had been a martial artist we would have cited him as an Immortal. Basically, these were guys who cultivated the internal energies of their bodies. They opened up the central channel. They got the microcosmic circulation, the River Chariot going, and then the macrocosmic circulation, and then they went on to cultivate mental abilities, called samadhi attainments, and super powers from there.

Most people who tread these roads almost always end up using breathing methods of some type. Whatever their type of practice, it's almost always mixed with anapana and pranayama. At the higher stages, they always practice anapana and let the body transform on its own. You don't need to practice pranayama anymore at the high stages but you need it at the early stages to try to force some channels into opening. As to anapana, you use anapana to open up chi channels and detach from the body's energies; you shine awareness on them, being aware of them without grabbing them, so that all the channels open naturally without force.

The people who can open up their channels and transform their five elements at this level can do miraculous things, such as move at super human speeds. In the martial arts movies, you can see them climb high walls. They can use inner energies for attack, though of course at that level they have no need to do so because they usually avoid the karma of fighting. They can make body doubles. All sorts of paranormal effects are possible.

People say, "Well, this is all nonsense," but it's not nonsense. It's just that regular people don't know the principles behind these things, aren't familiar with cultivation, aren't cultivating themselves to even know there is a thing called chi, and don't meet anybody who's cultivating to these stages. There's a book called "Nothing Ever Happened" by a Hindu sage Papaji, and he talks about meeting someone like this who achieved these abilities just from his yoga cultivation.

When you read his modern book, you know that Papaji (H.W.L. Poonja) is not a liar about anything. In his travels he meets a young guy who had learned to levitate, and demonstrated this attainment. He could make body doubles, speak in any language, and said he could travel to other worlds ... all the things that Taoists tell you that you can do with sufficient practice. He could achieve these things because he started practicing when he was young, practiced celibacy for the necessary stages, and he learned how to cultivate his internal energies through meditation.

It's always better to start cultivating these things when you're younger than when you're older because you have more vitality, but no one ever hands you this information and the key ingredients as we're discussing in this book. In any case, you can accomplish this sort of thing if you set your mind to it; you just have to ask whether it's worthy of you. The Indian yoga schools always talk about these abilities and catalogue many such super powers which they call **siddhis**.

There are eight siddhis in particular that you can cultivate, such as being able to reduce your body to a tiny size, or make it very large, or very heavy. I've seen martial artists who have cultivated that one in particular, but not to the extent capable from mastering *nei-gong*. They kneel on the ground, and you can't lift them up or move them. Another siddhi is that you can become weightless, and there are all sorts of other possible abilities like that.

There's another book called "Sky Dancer" about Yeshe Tsogyel, who was a female meditation practitioner in Tibet who was cultivating a lot of the form practices of Tibetan Buddhism. In this book, which describes her life story, there was a very big dharma battle between the priests of the Bon religion and the accomplished Tibetan Buddhists. It doesn't make sense to have a dharma battle unless we are talking about realized practitioners.

In any case, the Tibetan Buddhists won hands down, but during this battle a lot of the adepts ended up showing their super powers in order that the Buddhist side would win, like being able to run like the wind, walk on water, project things you could see into the sky, or summoning animals.

All these abilities were the special martial arts attainments you read about and everyone goes after. They became possible due to mastering specific samadhi that pertained to specific functional attainments or masteries, as introduced by the discussion on kasina concentrations. The relevant section runs as follows:

> Then the time arrived for the competition in evidence of *siddhi* [supernormal abilities]. Vairotsana held the three realms in the palm of his hand. Namkhai Nyingpo, riding on the sun's rays, demonstrated many miracles. Sangye Yeshe summoned malevolent spirits with a gesture of his purbha, slew his enemies with a movement of his phurba, and pierced a stone with a thrust of his phurba [just as in the Story of King Arthur]. Dorje Dunjom ran like the wind, encircling the four continents in a flash, and offered the King seven different kinds of treasure as proof of his feat. Gyelwa Chokyang projected Hayagriva, the Horse-necked, from his fontanelle, instantaneously filling the microcosmic universes with the sound of his neighing. Tsang-ri Gompo conquered the three realms in an instant, and offered the god Brahma's nine-spoked wheel as proof of his feat. Gyelwa Lodro walked on water. Denma Tsemang conclusively defeated the Bon in religious debate, explaining the *Kanjur Rochok* from memory, projecting the forms of the vowels and consonants into the sky. Kaba Peltsek enslaved the legions of arrogant spirits. Odren Zhonnu swam like a fish in the ocean. Jnana Kumara drew ambrosia from a rock. Ma Rinchen Chok ate pebbles, chewing them like dough. Pelgyi Dorje moved unimpeded through rocks and mountains. Sokpo Lhapel summoned a female tiger in heat from the south by means of his hook-*mudra*, his *mantra* of summons and his *samadhi*. Drenpa Namkha summoned a wild yak from the north. Chokro Lui Gyeltsen invoked the manifest forms of the Three Lords of the Buddha's Three Aspects in the sky in front of him. Langdro Konchok Jungden brought down thirteen thunderbolts at once, and dispatched them like arrows wherever he wished. Kyeuchung caught and bought all the Dakinis with his *samadhi*. Gyelmo Yudra Nyingpo disciplined the Bon in grammar, logic and science, and overpowering external appearances through the penetrating insight of his *samadhi*, he effected many transformations. Gyelwa Jangchub levitated in lotus posture. Tingdzin Zangpo flew in the sky, his vision encompassing the four continents simultaneously. In this manner all of the Twenty-five Mahasiddhas of Chimphu demonstrated evidence of their *siddhi* [attained through the practice of dhyana]. Furthermore, the Eight Siddhas of Yerpa, the

Thirty Tantric Priests of Sheldrak, the Fifty-five Recluses of Yong Dzong, etc., all showed a particular dissimilar sign of *siddhi*. They transmuted fire into water and water into fire. They danced in the sky, passed unimpeded through mountains and rocks, walked on water, reduced many to a few and increased a few into a multitude [like Jesus' feeding of the loaves of Bread to the multitude]. All the Tibetan people could not help but gain great faith in the Buddha, and the Bon could not help their defeat. The Bonpo ministers amongst the ministers were speechless.

Concerning the details of my contest with the Bon in evidence of *siddhi* the Bon were defeated. But afterwards they wove nine evil spells called The Magical Odour of the Skunk, Flinging Food to the Dog, Snuffing the Butter Lamp with Blood, Black Magical Leather, Projection of Pestilential Spirits and Projection of Devils, etc. With these curses they struck down nine young monks at once, but I spat into each of the monks' mouths, so that they stood up fully restored, showing greater skill in the play of wisdom than before. Thus again the Bon were defeated. Then pointing my index finger in gesture of threat at the nine magicians, and incanting PHAT! Nine times over, paralysed, they lost consciousness. To restore them I intoned HUNG nine times. Levitating in lotus posture, etc., I demonstrated my full control over elemental forces. Spinning fire wheels of five colours in the tips of the fingers of my right hand, I terrified the Bon, and then ejecting streams of five-coloured water from the tips of the fingers of my left hand, the streams swirled away into a lake. Taking a Chimphu boulder, breaking it like butter, I moulded it into various images. Then I projected twenty-five apparitional forms similar to myself, each displaying some proof of *siddhi*. [*Sky Dancer*, Keith Dowman (Sow Lion Publications, Ithaca: New York, 1996), pp. 112-113.]

These things are not impossible but once again, if you don't get to the genuine stage of *nei-gong* and then *Tao-gong*, you can't do them at all. You cannot even approach them, and so they'll seem fictional. If a martial artist proceeds along the martial arts road of practice and then cultivates *nei-gong* and then samadhi, they can demonstrate this sort of thing, and we thus put this in the category of internal martial arts. If the individual who cultivates is not a martial artist but achieves them, then we simply call it spiritual attainments. What people don't get is that the two are the same, and you are simply approaching the attainments from two different roads of practice, as I explained earlier – the "Buddhist" or "Taoist."

If you want to know what the genuine stage of opening the chi channels entails, which lays a foundation for the real *nei-gong* and samadhi attainments enabling these things, you've got to read the "Little Book of Hercules" and then do all the preliminary practices to get there. The preliminary practices always involve pranayama and they usually involve the white skeleton visualization practice, or some other tantric visualization involving the chi channels and chakras of the body.

Usually they use a skeleton visualization of some type, which is why you see, in many schools, pictures of skeletons. You'll see this in Tibetan Buddhism. You'll see it in the Greek myths. You'll see this in countless traditions because you usually will see various visions when you pass through certain stages of *nei-gong* cultivation. When you are transforming the dense earth element of the body, which is transforming the skeleton chi of the body, that's when you'll see visions of skeletons. It means that the earth chi of your body is being transformed.

If you don't do the preliminary practices that prepare you for entering into these accomplishments, it's impossible to do these things. You can do some amazing things, for sure, but not really the super powers at these levels of achievement. You need internal cultivation and samadhi attainments to get that far. As stated, you have to go from the external martial arts through chi cultivation to internal energy cultivation (wherein you totally transform your physical nature) and then to *Tao-gong* cultivation to become able to do these things. Even *nei-gong* alone won't usually cut it. That's the secret. It's not that this is impossible, but that few ever bother to cultivate this far.

Once again, basically the principle is that these special feats are possible, but only if somebody really starts succeeding in *nei-gong*. And that's really the big principle that people don't know. How do you get there? Well, you have to start with martial arts so that you get healthy. And then you have to go through the *qi-gong* route, which is to get you to the stage where you start feeling the chi of your body. And then you must make progress in the various practices such as meditation, anapana, pranayama and visualization. If you learn how to let go of your thoughts from these practices, and let go of your mind, your chi will rise. You'll start opening up the channels and chakras within your body, and you'll start being able to enter into this pathway.

If you don't do that however, then it's never going to happen no matter how hard you try and how hard you visualize. That's really the main thing that a lot of martial artists don't know. They see some of these special abilities fictionalized in cartoons like "Naruto" and "Dragonball Z," and they wish they could do some of them. They believe and yet they don't believe. Once again, you've got to get to the stage of *nei-gong* and then cultivate the samadhi of *Tao-gong* and then all sorts of supernormal abilities become possible, but not necessarily the ones you see on TV.

On a mundane level, one of the more mythic martial arts abilities is *Dim Mak* where a martial artist can touch someone at a certain spot and either kill them with the touch, or knock them out, or freeze them or whatever. This type of practice is unusual, but is still in the realm of mundane achievements even though it requires skill, practice, and internal energy cultivation.

My teacher, when he was younger, was invited to learn this. There was a little town in China that basically had its own traditional knowledge of how to do this martial arts skill. There are many different martial arts schools in China and a lot of them have hometowns with special traditions. My teacher had been the martial arts champion of all eighteen weapons for his entire province, and a representative of this town came to him and said, "We want you to learn this because we only teach it to one person per generation, and we think you can do it." My teacher was interested, of course, and asked them how long it would take and they said, "This takes several years to learn and master." And he said, "Well, I'd love to learn it, but I don't have that many years because I have another mission in my life that I want to do." So he had to pass on that.

Such things as *Dim Mak* are possible. He knew I was interested in learning about this skill, so once he sent me into China to see a psychologist who was trying to take what he had read of those ancient traditions and then reestablish them in Chinese culture. They're shown in all the martial arts movies, but people have lost the original teachings, so this man wanted to try and reconstruct them, and see if he could use them in a useful way.

And so I was there with three friends in the room with this psychologist and his diluted version of *Dim Mak*, and he started using this methodology he had reinvented on a patient, which involved just mild pressure on some points on the chest and arm – the exact points I don't remember clearly. When he started doing that on his patient, who was sitting on a chair, one of my companions standing in the room just fainted due to the energies. I actually thought she was faking because he wasn't working on her at all, but in any case I had to catch her as she fell. Perhaps it was because of the energies involved since she was very sensitive, but in any case I had to catch her and make her lie down, and that was just from seeing the demonstration. I didn't feel anything, and it had absolutely no effect on me at all.

So there is stuff like that out there in the world that still works, and which doesn't require a lot of *nei-gong* cultivation but just the right knowledge of pressure points, acupuncture meridians and so forth. You still must do a lot of training and practice to learn skills like that, and usually such skills die away because no one wants to practice them anymore or no one wants to teach them, so I'm hoping this little book provides enough insights to help martial arts blow open this field of internal energy, even though it's dangerous to go down that pathway without a wise teacher. That's another issue entirely because I think my view on the physical form cultivation schools is well known. If you don't have the right view or right understanding, it's dangerous to pursue these routes because individuals usually get fascinated by all the powers they can develop, and thereby get lost and distracted from the big picture. Or, they just hurt themselves with the energies they release unless they do a lot of preparatory cultivation work ahead of time.

There are a lot of skills like *Dim Mak* that take a lot of time to learn as well as the cultivation of inner power. And it's just an issue in your life that you have to say to yourself, "Well, I only have so many years to live. What do I want to master before it's over? What do I want to learn with my valuable time?" Because *nei-gong* leads to *Tao-gong*, this route is highly commendable, but just to learn a super power or skill for no reason at all, you really have to rethink it.

There's a famous story of the monk Xuan Zang from China which brings up this same issue. The whole book "The Journey to the West" is a fictional account written about this monk who went to ancient India to bring the Buddhist sutras back to China. When he was there he met one of the students or grand students of the Esoteric master Nagarjuna. Nagarjuna, who was the real founder of the Esoteric school of Buddhism, was said to have lived for a couple of hundred years, and this student was said to have already lived for a couple of hundred years, too.

Xuan Zang said, "Gee, I'd like to learn how to do that." And the student said, "You're welcome to it, but you're going to have to change your body and learn medicine for the first ten to twelve years to do so." Xuan Zang said, "Well, I'm going to have to pass on this opportunity then because I vowed to bring all these sutras back to China, so I have to get back to China with all of them, and I can't spend that many years here." As explained in "The Little Book of Hercules" and "Measuring Meditation," this is how long it takes to really open up your chi channels and transform your chi to establish a good physical foundation for the physical attainments of the Tao.

Another story concerns my teacher and an Immortal swordsman. My teacher tracked this man down in Hangzhou at the time, and asked this master to show him his accomplished "flying sword" technique where you can project cutting energies at a distance. The master brushed him off several times, but because of his sincerity he finally brought his top student out and said, "Watch this." The student took in a deep breath, held it, and then forcefully expelled it from his nostrils. Puffs of dust arose from the ground where two holes started to form in the dirt. This was due to the energies released from his nostrils that hit the earth below.

My teacher said along the lines of, "That's fine, but I really want to see your flying sword technique," because at that time he was young and interested in all sorts of martial arts gong-fu. China was fighting a war with Japan, and my teacher felt that if he knew how to do this, he could just sit there and flick his hand and cut the tails off the Japanese planes in the sky so that they'd fall to the ground. This is always the type of idea a twenty year old has, but you never see people at this sort of level doing anything like that, so you have to ask yourself why. In any case, the master swordsman took him to the top of a hill and pointed to a set of trees across the way, and told everyone to watch the tops of the trees in the distance. He then pointed at them with a swing, generating a slicing bolt of invisible chi, and the tops of the trees immediately fell off.

When my teacher asked him to teach him the method, the Immortal swordsman said he didn't want to fill his mind with all sorts of busy nonsense. He kept telling him not to fill his mind with more and more things, but to start letting go, for emptiness was more important than this sort of skill. "Don't waste your precious time trying to learn this sort of thing," he said, "but cultivate the great void instead."

He somehow knew my teacher was talented in that direction and so he was trying to tell him that it was better to spend his time cultivating the Tao than trying to accumulate all these skills. In life you have to choose what you'll cultivate with the little time you have. The supreme cultivation achievement is to realize the Tao, and then finish off the body cultivation, after which all these skills come much easier. Martial arts is a great way of getting your body half way there, then switching to Tao cultivation, and then coming back to finish it up. But if you remain wholly fixed on cultivating the body, that's the only achievement you'll have.

Ultimately, there are a lot of things you can put your energies into through training and practice and time. And you just have to ask yourself, "Is it worthy of me?" Because there are methods in India where you can go into a pit for several years and learn how to create fire by thought or by touching something. And it might take you ten years to learn how to do that, to harness the power of the sun with certain mantras and whatever. But you have to ask yourself, "Is it worthwhile to spend ten years of my life learning how to do that or can I just buy a cigarette lighter and have a fire wherever I want? Is it wise to spend twenty years learning how to walk on water, or can I just hire a boat when I need one?"

This all gets back to the idea of training. If you're a martial artist, there's a book that I highly recommend that you read which is not about martial arts, but about training. I don't care how long you've been practicing martial arts and what school or tradition you follow, but you should read this book called "The Talent Code" and recommend it to your friends, because the knowledge within it will have a great bearing on your practice and thus skills.

6

MODERN TRAINING SECRETS FOR PERFECTING ANCIENT SKILLS

"The Talent Code," by Daniel Coyle, is a special book that all martial artists should read, and which all martial arts teachers should make their students read. There are three other books with similar content that basically say, "It doesn't matter what your initial level of talent is, it's how much you practice that counts," and that's the message of this book.

They are finding that this conclusion is true for all fields of endeavor. Sports, music, dance, stock trading, ... world class expertise comes down to either ten years of practice or 10,000 hours of deep practice done in a particular, special way. If you want more on this topic there's "The Bounce," "Talent is Overrated," and "Outliers" but the best of the lot is "The Talent Code."

The idea of this book is that if you repeat a skill over and over and over again, myelin insulation will build up around the nerve circuits in the brain and body that will be activated by that skill, so you always want to repeat your martial arts forms correctly from the start, *and in a slow fashion*, so that you are practicing in the right way.

If you practice in the wrong way, myelin will build up around those wrong circuits, and then it will be difficult to change those habits once they are ingrained in deep myelin coatings. If you practice correctly over time, however, you're going to create new circuits – the correct ones. If you do it over and over and over again for 10,000 hours, you can develop a world class skill.

Researchers have consistently found this result in music, in sports, in dance, in stock trading, in painting ... in any field. If you do "deep practice" like this for 10,000 hours, you can develop world class skills, and that includes skills for martial arts. Hence, you can see the benefits of starting young. If you started martial arts when you were six years old, by the time you're a teenager, if you were practicing every year, you're definitely through to expert territory if you really went with it.

If you start at age twenty and you keep working at it and you put the "10,000 hours" in, then however long it takes after that, you can also develop a world class skill. It doesn't matter when you start, though of course, earlier is better than later for a large number of reasons. It just takes training and practice hours.

This ties in with the idea of sports psychology, peak performance training and flow. The whole idea is that talent is not born, but it's grown. I don't care what your level is at martial arts right now. If you just keep practicing and practicing and practicing, it will get better. That understanding can help someone maintain their commitment to years of training and practice to where they can finally reach a high level of competence. You need that understanding. And usually, the 10,000 hours turns into ten years of practice, but it can be less time, too.

The whole idea within this concept of practice is that you have to break a skill into component pieces, like when you are memorizing a routine or circuit. You memorize the individual pieces. You practice each of those pieces until it's correct. You don't move on to other pieces until you get the prior pieces of the circuit correct. And you practice slowly, correctly, so that you really get it down and the myelin and nerve circuits build up around that correct movement or form. Furthermore, you can add visualization into the mix, which will really help you with your mastery of a movement.

You should never keep practicing something wrong because then you're building up this myelin sheath and ingrained habit for the wrong pattern. You practice until something is correct and then you link the pieces together into progressively larger groups, and that's it. You only practice what's right, not wrong, and you always *slow down to catch the errors* so that you're practicing always what's right.

This often explains why if you watch boxing or MMA or any of the fighting, they'll have somebody who is obviously a very well trained fighter. But for some reason, they always do some stupid thing, like they keep their hands too low so their face is open. They always do that no matter how many times someone tells them not to because they've been training wrong and now it's hard to correct the bad habit, which was an incorrect form from the start. They've built the circuit in their brain to do it wrong because they didn't train correctly, and now it's hard to unlearn it.

If someone had introduced this idea and this book "The Talent Code" to me when I was young, everything would be totally different in my life. I'm the type of person who needs explanations, as most Westerners do, and this supplies the reasons and motivation to work harder at your martial arts or other areas you want to master, and more carefully.

A lot of the people who are appearing on "American Idol," for instance, have been singing since they were young. But it floored me when I found out that many went to the same singing coach in Texas, Linda Septien, who basically ran them through certain exercises that made them into better singers. They put in those 10,000 hours. So people don't realize it, but in nearly every single field of endeavor this rule of mastery is universal.

"The Talent Code" is therefore a wonderful book to put in the reach of students when they are young so they understand the importance and role of practice, and why they have to practice correctly, and recognize that talent is built so that they don't become discouraged. If you're a martial arts teacher, go buy it so that you have the proof and explanations that will help you talk to your students and convince them to try harder, because the author goes through dozens and dozens of sports examples. You'll have the proof that you need to tell people that they have to keep practicing to a deep level.

The great quality about the book is that it dispenses with this idea of natural talent being necessary for superior performance. After reading this book you will never say to yourself again, "Oh, geez, I'm terrible. I just don't have the natural skill." That's the wrong idea. You just need to practice correctly, and for enough time, and then the skill will come. You have to break each skill into component pieces, practice each section slowly but perfectly, and then link them all together, and if you throw visualization of the movement into this type of practice, that will help.

To do that you might need to view a video recording of the movement done correctly and watch it over and over again, like watching someone's golf swing or tennis return until the movement penetrates into your subconscious, and in the case of visualization practice you visualize yourself doing it. The principle is slow practice/imitation of a perfect model, then perfect practice, then repeated perfect practice.

My teacher often told me the example where the worst guy in his own martial arts class was made a master in some town. He was shocked when he heard this and was perplexed. This guy was the lousiest one in his class, and no one could have predicted this outcome.

My own teacher went to visit him and said something akin to, "What happened that all these people take you as their master? What gives?" And the guy said, "Well, hit me with this pole." When my teacher tried to hit him with a pole, his friend put up his arm to block it, and his arm broke the pole.

He then said, "Well, I realized I wasn't that talented. Therefore, what I did was I just kept hitting my arm with chopsticks and then other devices every day (a practice known as *pai da*) to build up the chi flow through the area, all the time increasing the number of hits and number of hard items I used to strengthen my muscles and bones. I basically took that to a skill level where it became something where I can break everything without feeling any pain. So, now they consider me a master."

This is a textbook example of traditional Iron Shirt training method where you start by gently hitting the part of the body you want to be able to resist strikes. Over time you move systematically from tiny sticks, to bigger sticks, to rods and so forth. It is considered a lower form of Iron Shirt largely because of the damage it does to the body, but many martial artists have used these methods to develop fists that can punch through anything, and Mui Thai Boxers use it to develop hard shins for kicking and so.

Most of these martial artists realize too late that the natural consequence of this lower method is to suffer early onset of arthritis, loss of movement in the joints and other negative side effects. This is another reason why you have to learn about the existence of various bodywork modalities, or supplements for the joints such as pharmaceutical grade glucosamine sulfate, Super Cissus, HylaRub hyaluronic acid, or even gin soaked yellow raisins. Too many martial artists, especially in judo, karate, and the other hard schools of practice, really damage their knees or shoulder joints unless they know how to practice correctly and fix problems before they become permanent disabilities. So I've given you plenty of indications for that which you won't normally encounter such as Z-Health, bodywork and special supplements.

The higher form of Iron Shirt practice is when it moves to *qi-gong* and then *nei-gong*, where rather than damaging a part of the body to make it stronger the practitioner uses his mind to move chi to an area to protect it – which has the added benefit of helping to open up the channels in that area and increase your health as well as your martial arts ability.

There are lots of different types of martial arts that you see over and over again in the movies, and it's simply because somebody took an exercise and they did it in the right way, so they didn't hurt themselves, and they built up internal energy and applied it to the exercise. They basically kept practicing for so many hours that they developed a special skill or excellence that, when we see it, we go "Wow! That's amazing." It might have initially started from just a tiny smidgeon or even non-existence of the specific talent, but the final excellence is all due to deep practice.

It's like Iron Palm martial arts training routines where you practice slow, gentle exercises of slapping the surface of water or a bucket of beans, sand or iron with your palm, all the while keeping your mind on your hand. In conjunction with breathing exercises developed to help push chi to the hands, you do this every day. If you keep your mind on your palm as you slowly exercise it this way, the chi capabilities of the palm build up slowly over a long period of time and because it wasn't forced, the chi becomes able to freely flow to this part of the body. If you do this incorrectly, your hand develops calluses. If you do it correctly, your hands will stay normal looking or even become softer, like a woman's hands, and yet you'll still be able to penetrate several bricks with a slap. Your capabilities all depend on the slow, deliberate, eventual buildup of chi cultivation. If you are too eager or stubborn in your approach, you will develop health problems.

Many skills of internal gong-fu, like Iron Palm and Iron Shirt, Golden Bell Cover and *Dim Mak* can be developed if you keep at it. You can always develop special abilities if you keep at it. However, the skills of localized gong-fu often dissipate in later years unless you learn internal gong-fu, meditation and so forth. If you don't learn meditation, *qi-gong* and then *nei-gong*, you will never perfect your gong-fu to the highest levels possible.

In any case, part of this achievement is practice, so how to keep the spirit of practice alive? Through motivation, inspiration and also by telling people to read "The Talent Code" so that they understand its importance.

I also always tell people, "If you're young, there are three movies that are fantastic for teaching this principle of the necessity for deep practice for attaining gong-fu."

The first movie is Jackie Chan's "Drunken Master." If you've seen it, you'll probably remember the scene where he does sit-ups hanging upside down, filling up a bucket of water with tiny cups. Almost every young kid getting started in martial arts remembers that scene because they're like, "Oh my god!" But that's the type of devoted practice that you need to do.

For instance, few people can stand in a semi horse stance with arms extended for several minutes, let alone 30-60 minutes or several hours, and yet that's what builds up your abilities in Tai Chi and other martial arts. What takes place on an external and internal level as you do this is no different than what most people experience as they go through the pain of learning cross-legged sitting meditation. Your mind hurts, your body hurts, and you question why you are doing this and even cry. These are all natural reactions, and you just have to keep practicing and go through it. Whether you are practicing the horse stance or the lotus position, maintaining these positions helps to open up the chi routes within your body. The longer you can hold them, the more your channels will open, but of course you can only open them in a gradual fashion. If you try too much in one go you will certainly hurt yourself.

That idea of practice also comes across beautifully in another famous movie called "The 36th Chamber of Shaolin" or "Shaolin Master Killer" starring Liu Chia-Hui (Gordon Liu). It goes by several different names. It has highly fictionalized training sequences for various stages of Shaolin training. These training sequences are the really cool thing about the movie even though it's silly stuff. As a kid you see these strange training exercises corresponding to different stages – they're all fictional, mind you - and you're like, "Wow! There are stages of practice and I have to learn how to do them in sequence. I have to strengthen my arms by carrying buckets of water, learn how to step on floating logs without falling in the water, use my eyes instead of moving my head if I'm going to be a good martial artist," and so forth. In a way it's like the "Karate Kid" in that certain preparatory martial arts exercises are hidden in the daily life of the monks and their normal chores.

The whole idea is that you need a teacher and a slow training system that will put you through these practices for a long period of time, just like assuming the horse stance position for hours. That's going to build up the muscles you need strengthened, and it's going to help heal your body, too. If you do it wrong, if you practice wrong, you're screwed.

If you do it right, then you can be like Jet Li in the movie "Shaolin Temple," which is the third movie I always recommend. There's a wonderful scene in this movie – it's very brief but I love watching it over and over again because of its scenic beauty - where the seasons change from summer to winter to spring to fall and in each season they show Jet Li practicing. It's like a two-minute training scene where he's practicing a different martial art form during each of the seasons. It's very beautiful.

The whole idea once again, through these movies, is that you really just have to keep practicing correctly over time, and then you will slowly develop a skill to a high level of excellence. I don't want anybody to come to this idea that, "Well, this is all beyond me. I'm not skilled in martial arts or sports or athletics so I shouldn't even start." *Nei-gong* is the same way. Everyone can reach these stages. You just have to practice and keep at it. You start with meditation, anapana, visualization practice and move into it. It's like the movie "The Karate Kid" where you start out with zero knowledge of the subject. Everyone initially starts with a talent level of zero in this area.

After reviewing this book while in its preparatory stages, a martial arts teacher and friend, David Farmer, wrote me to say the following. This once again touches upon the importance of standing practice for opening up the energy channels in the legs, which is one of the secrets to developing real internal power for the martial arts:

In the old days, if an individual was allowed to become a martial arts student of a Master, usually the student performed mundane things for some time. Many times these useless chores designed by the Master allowed the unnoticing student to build kung fu [gong-fu].

Finally after some time, the Master instructed the student to be taught by one of his senior students. Most of the beginning exercises, as simple as they seem, are the most profound. An example is that students would spend many hours a day for many years doing nothing but standing still in different stances and postures. Standing exercises are more profound than one realizes. Students in the traditional martial arts didn't start out by learning a bunch of fancy forms. Everything was static. Standing meditation, as was taught, was one of those forms and must have a focal point. But this focal point was not taught in the beginning phase for students learning martial arts.

First a person had to learn how to stand, they had to learn the proper technique how to stand. Just like in sitting meditation, a person had to learn how to rest using their mind, the false mind of conception, in order to realize the real mind, the uncompounded mind and develop their chi. When one develops correctly, one rests the body on the perfectly aligned bones, the muscles remain neutral, the tendons in perfect poise, the monkey mind is tamed and great awareness has been brought to the forefront and remains as the birth and death of thoughts comes and goes. More importantly, the body has developed a lot of chi which flows unobstructed now. A person feels light, but appears very heavy so that many times by using thought they can prevent another person from pushing them off center.

Once a person could stand for long periods of time and their body stopped jerking around, they stopped bobbing back and forth, and they appeared quiet on the outside, they then would be taught the mental aspect of the stance. Within this new found peace they usually are taught to concentrate on their breathing. Just like in anapana practice they were taught to become aware and watch the breath, but not force their breath.

Much of what happens after this stage is just a natural spontaneous reaction of body, which must occur. We can only stop it from happening when we practice incorrectly. In time a person notices that their breath becomes very soft and penetrating. All this time their power of awareness becomes stronger, in that it notices the coming and going of wind and the coming and going of the occasional false thought. In time a practitioner falls away from awareness to just knowing or witnessing this whole process.

Many times during this process one's feet start to get warm, hot etc. My own feet developed red patches resembling blisters. In time this goes away and one finds more peace and witnesses more quiet knowing until it seems that with an inhale the pores of the skin open and with the exhale the pores close. Whole body breathing is a byproduct of a level that one attains in standing meditation.

All this time the Master is watching you, so by now he starts to give you a hand position to hold with the stance. What many martial artists don't realize is that most of these positions relate to a specific set of meridians or chi channels. Tradition holds that there are 108 positions that if practiced successfully work every channel in the body. The chi channels of the body can be cleaned by certain positions coupled with mental practice that, cultivated together, allow one to become an Immortal.

Only after having "10,000 hours" of practicing one posture, namely a lot, did you get taught another posture. This went on until you learned the 72 postures that made up one form, and only then did you get to link them together. Once you practiced the moving linkage you tried to hold on to the emptiness that one experiences in a static position. In the old days it was not hard for a monk to maintain this. Today, we see people running thru a form and they are all out of breath at the end.

I am not going to say that standing is harder than sitting meditation, only that one must throw themselves into the one that best suits them. It has been taught, that the faithful in the past would cultivate realization for tens of years, thru all kinds of hardships, but in the end they would need to conquer themselves standing, walking or lying down, which, in the end, requires meditation.

You cannot over-emphasize the importance of learning how to remain standing, in the proper posture or position, for hours at a time in order to increase your prowess and powerful abilities in martial arts. This alone will help you open up your leg meridians even without meditation practice, which is necessary for true *nei-gong*, though meditation will advance your practice yet further.

If you put in the practice with the proper technique over the right time with commitment, you'll eventually attain high gong-fu, but you must notice that there is a great mental component to the practice that very much sounds like meditation, only it is eventually linked with movement. Now, if you don't put in the right time and you don't put in the right exercise and effort, you're never going to get the targeted end results. It doesn't mean that the special abilities and the gong-fu don't exist. It just means you haven't worked hard enough and gotten to that level.

There's a martial arts story that reminds me of this principle, and which ties into the idea of the 10,000 hours we've been talking about, which is basically the idea of repetition. If you want to learn something, and learn it well, you must train yourself through sufficient repetition and you must concentrate on the basics. The basics, for *nei-gong*, start with hours of *wai-gong* standing practice to help open up the foot channels. Standing practice is like holding a yoga asana posture for a long period of time, only you are standing straight up. This practice generates lots of power, and has untold benefits if you learn how to do it correctly and can hold it for a long period of time.

They say the secret is in the basics, and the basics include standing practice to help open up the foot channels, as well as for a wide variety of other reasons as well. If you want great martial arts, do lots of standing practice so you can hold a horse stance for hours, if possible. In any case, while it refers to karate, this story from businessman Chet Holmes once again brings home the importance of constant training starting from "skill level zero" to master a skill:

> When I was 15 years old, I tried a new method for increasing my karate skills. I had a high vaulted ceiling in my bedroom. I screwed a cowhide rope into the peak of the ceiling and attached a softball to the other end, at chest level. My intent was to kick and chop the ball and then to be able to deflect it, block it, kick it, or chop the ball again when it came bouncing back.
>
> With my first karate chop at the ball with my hand, the ball bounced out to the edge of the rope and back fast, smacking me in the head.

This wasn't going to be as easy as I thought. I tried all kinds of kicks – hook kick, front kick, back kick, side kick – but again and again the ball flew to the end of the rope and then bounced back, hitting me in the head, elbow, shoulders or chest.

I worked on this for several weeks and made very little progress. After a month, there were a couple of times when I could actually clock the ball from hitting me. After three months of doing this every single day, I could hit the ball with any one of the body's weapons – my hands, my feet, my elbows, and my knees. I could even do a spinning back kick and hit it again, then block it expertly as it flew at me from a different angle.

After six months, the ball never touched me. I could spin artfully in the air, flawlessly blocking the ball at every angle. It was amazing. I could literally catch, kick or swat the ball with every move any time I liked and faster than I would've ever thought possible. My body was operating like a machine, responding to the ball as if preprogrammed to anticipate every possible move the ball could make.

Imagine my skill level when that ball would ricochet around the room with lightning speed and my reflexes were even faster. It was thrilling. I felt such power. I realized that becoming a master of karate was not about learning 4,000 moves but about doing just a handful of moves 4,000 times. [*The Ultimate Sales Machine*, Chet Holmes, (Penguin Group, New York, 2007), p. xix.]

This is the big, big lesson that I want people to learn which either nobody ever bothers to tell them, or just isn't stressed enough. I don't care what you want to learn, but don't hop from technique to technique until you put hours and hours into mastering the basics. You'll find this idea explained in "The Talent Code" for many areas of life. Pick up "The Talent Code" which you can get on amazon.com, and it will really help your progress.

Another story that comes to mind, related to this, was told to me by a friend who had a martial arts teacher from China. This man could move at lightning speeds, and he explained it was because he had done special exercises for his ribs and upper torso.

It's hard in martial arts to connect the energies of the upper torso with those below on through to the legs so that the top and bottom half of the body are integrated. Most schools focus on the movements of the waist, and generally neglect the chest somewhat. I'm told that this man, using the model of a tiger whose entire chest cavity of ribs moves when it breathes, mastered the ability to contract his ribs and generate a power from the chest cavity that most people never cultivate. It's a forgotten skill in martial arts and takes years of training and practice to be able to do this.

To train, I'm told that every day he would extend his hand into a contraption he had built that was like a clothes hanger on a stretchable, elastic cord that hung from the ceiling. It would hang directly in front of him at the level of his outstretched arm. Every day he would extend his arm so that the wrist rested in this holder, and he would try to move it downwards just by contracting his ribs alone, and without using any other muscles. Naturally he did all sorts of other exercises to loosen the connective tissues around his ribs, and eventually he developed tremendous abilities from this practice. This involved cultivating his muscles, breathing and internal energies all together.

He taught the basics to my friend and lamented, as I mentioned earlier, that no one in China wanted to learn this type of martial arts because it took too long. No one wanted to practice by putting in the time and commitment. He could not find a single Chinese who wanted to learn the tradition, and had found that only Americans were interested in this type of learning, yet he couldn't find anyone to transmit it to before he died. Everyone wanted just simple stuff you could learn quickly, or wanted large variety of flashy techniques without learning any of them well, so he could not find anyone for the transmission.

Once again, for really great achievement you must understand that it comes down to slow, deliberate, steady practice of the right form performed in the right way. I cannot find a better example than this one of how long it might take to learn something, and yet you can do it if you set your mind to it.

In addition to this idea of practice, there are several little known disciplines I'd like to introduce that can help people achieve a higher level of physical practice. There are a couple of different things that are really wonderful for your martial arts practice which few people know about.

For the joints of the body and maximizing their flexibility and degrees of motion, I think the **Z-Health videos** (www.zhealth.net), which are based on the flexibility training work of Scott Sonnon, are fantastic. One of my pet peeves about the American educational system when it comes to sports and athletics is that a lot of what we teach cannot be practiced as people get older, and that's when people need to keep moving and need exercise the most. Tai Chi, yoga, and Z-Health are things you can find seniors doing that keep the joints and muscles active and help eliminate aches and pains, but instead we put all this emphasis on team sports that you can only play in your younger years, and you need team participation as well. What's that going to do for you when you are old?

I would want my children to be introduced to a type of exercise that is simple and becomes second nature to them so that when they're older they can pick it up again, and have no qualms about doing so from fearing it is too new and strange (such as how many people view yoga if they weren't introduced to it when young). Z-Health falls into that category, and it really is fantastic for helping to heal the joint injuries that martial artists suffer, *many of whom, through its use, can once again enter into and win world class competitions at a higher skill level than before they were injured.*

It only takes about ten minutes to practice this per day, where you basically put each of your joints through a simple circular range of motion exercise with three repetitions. This is easy to add to your routine, and you just do that every day. After a year, it's incredible what this does for your mobility, your flexibility, and it helps heal injuries, too. If you want to improve your martial arts skills, it's incredibly simple, easy, and super effective in ways I cannot describe. You just have to keep at it with the principles of deep practice.

I have not seen it or tried it and therefore cannot evaluate it, but for stretching some people tell me they like the work of **Lou Gross** (www.backfixbodywork.com) for connective tissues, and there are many other such teachers. The important point is that for stretching and issues with your connective tissues or muscle problems, a lot of martial artists are never introduced to the idea that you should go to a body worker now and then. That's the principle I want you to know. I always tell them, "Go to your local health food store, and find a good chiropractor and muscular bodyworker from their boards or ask other sports people, and visit them for a session."

Nine out of ten people in any professional aren't really that great so it always takes a while to find a really good chiropractor or bodyworker to put your bones in the right structural position, and help realign connective tissues. You have to find one through someone who has tried many, because if you've tried two dozen or more you can tell who's good, but most people have only tried two or three, and so their opinions don't really count as much (because from lack of extensive experience they therefore don't really know). That's one of the rules to pass on – ask people for their opinion if they have done something a lot, and tried different techniques, and you'll usually get a better answer than someone who has only done it a little.

For instance, I feel that one of the top chiropractors in the entire USA is Alex Belfer, who works in Brooklyn (New York City), and having used several dozen osteopaths, chiropractors and bone setters, I genuinely know who is good and who is not. Alex can definitely help people with structural problems due to skeletal issues (polarity@optonline.net), so I always recommend him to those with serious troubles. Tim Ferris' book, "The 4-Hour Body: An Uncommon Guide to Rapid Fat Loss, Incredible Sex, and Becoming Superhuman," also contains some references for top bodywork practitioners who specialize in helping to fix physical injuries.

If your bones are structurally misaligned, your muscles are going to be too taut in some places and you're not going to get the highest level of martial arts excellence possible because your body is not in its natural state. First fix the bones, meaning their structural alignment, and then you can use bodywork for your tendons, muscles and connective tissues such as **IMT** or **Rolfing, Egoscue,** and so forth. There are lots of different bodywork therapies that I always recommend people go check out for their conditions, and of course you can also practice yoga, Pilates and Feldenkrais Therapy to help stretch your muscles and learn how to align yourself with gravity during your natural movements.

The first thing to check when you are having troubles with a form or stance is to check your skeletal alignment, and if you have aches and pains you should not just check your muscles but your skeletal alignment as well. Only then, after that is fixed, should you go to acupuncture and other techniques because everything is stretched across the framework of the bones. You have to get that right, first. It's hard to align all the parts of your body properly, or learn a movement correctly, if the skeleton is not aligned or the joints are damaged and causing pain or have restricted ranges of motion.

It's amazing how many people in the martial arts, especially in the hard martial arts like judo and karate, damage their knees and their shoulder joints whereby they have to go to an Egoscue therapist or IMT practitioner or somebody else to fix it. They don't even know that these bodywork methodologies are available to help heal injuries because nobody tells them, but the idea of going to bodyworkers is something that should go hand in hand with martial arts training and practice.

If you need to find a basic bodywork practitioner in your area, there's also a $10 directory called the "**International Association of Healthcare Practitioners Directory**" which lists who is available and what their skills are in each area code of the country, or you can search online at www.IAHP.com. There are usually dozens of practitioners listed per region, so there's always someone within a few miles of your home. If I don't have any personal recommendations from anyone for a city, I always recommend that you start looking for a practitioner by picking someone from the directory who is listed as having undergone lots of trainings (all their trainings are listed), as – with nothing else to go on - a larger number of trainings suggests they have lots of skill and experience.

I also always tell people to order a basic, or basic and advanced Z-Health CD video, and do the simple daily rotational routines for their joints, and try to do connective tissue stretching before trainings. This alone will help your martial arts get to the next level, which is another of the purposes of this small book. Z-Health is a million dollar tip for you in terms of structural mechanics of movement, and increasing the range of motion of your joints.

You have to think outside the box and tap into different techniques and methods to reach a higher standard of excellence where you become the best in your field. For instance, Arnold Schwarzenegger learned ballet in order to win some Mr. Olympia championships because it helped him make his movements more graceful as he switched from posing position to position. He said to himself, "How am I going to win Mr. Olympia and all these contests unless I learn how to be more graceful? Ballet will do it." Regardless as to what his he-man friends would say, he wanted to win competitions so he started to learn ballet. A lot of people don't know that.

His competitors in bodybuilding would never have done this at that time in history, thinking it unmanly, but Schwarzenegger was smart enough to realize this extra training would help him, so he went on to using this different modality from an entirely new tradition just as he had used visualization practice. That's an idea I'm trying to teach you, too, which is to take up visualization practice to make your training time shorter.

If you really want better martial arts skills, then borrow, benchmark, cross-research, and take from whatever else might help you, whether its pranayama or visualization or Z-Health or supplements or whatever. For a while there, a lot of pro football teams were having their linemen practice ballet movements, too. These big 350 or 400-pound linemen were doing ballet to get more graceful and increase their agility, too.

There are all sorts of techniques you can use to get better at martial arts. Recently I was sent a piece of equipment that had blinking lights on a pole, and you had to sit still and watch this beam as the lights blinked, without moving your head, to learn how to increase your visual acuity and widen your field of vision. It sort of reminded me of the scene in "36th Chamber of Shaolin" where Gordon Liu (Liu Chia-Hui), playing the monk San Te, had to stick his head between sticks of burning incense or metal spikes – I don't remember which it was - and learn how to extend the peripheral vision of his eyes without moving his head. There are all sorts of equipment, techniques and modalities available to help improve little things like this in your practice, and then of course it comes down to the training to use them and master them.

There's even a best selling Clickbank ebook out there on how you can learn how to jump higher, "The Jump Manual," by Jacob Hiller. There are all sorts of techniques today for peak performance in athletics and sports because of scientific studies on "what is best," and I'm sure you have seen TV programs on some of these things. We've got studies on the science of body mechanics and martial arts that involve all sorts of things except one – real *nei-gong*.

What you've got to do is find the expert for what you want to excel at and then learn their method, model it or duplicate it as the field of NLP (neuro-linguistic programming) would tell you to do, and then practice, practice, practice, and link it smoothly to all the other stuff that you're doing. But if your body structure is off because of the bones being out of alignment, then you'll have muscle and connective tissue issues that will affect your ability to duplicate a form with grace and execute the movement in the proper manner.

Most people who go through martial arts end up hurting their bodies and they can't move their bodies in certain ways because of damage or the fact that their structure is misaligned. So here's a big hint that a lot of people don't know about. Your body is going to try to protect, in a certain order, various structures within it. The primary thing that your body is going to do is it's going to try to protect its arteries, then its bones, then its veins, then its nerves, then the internal organs, then your lymph system, then the joints and the muscles *in that general order*. There is a ranking of priority for the things that need protection, and your muscles are at the bottom of the list. Your body will sacrifice your muscles to protect arteries, bones, veins, joints and so on, so you have to know how to fix the muscles by fixing all these other things through bodywork, supplements, or even meditation.

Take your arteries for instance. Your arteries are like tubes, they're like a telephone line which can get twisted. If your arteries get wound up with tension, then they might rip or suffer from micro tears if suddenly pulled. Cholesterol is there to patch some of the holes, but your body will tighten muscles to protect an artery that is already stretched too much.

Let's take your carotid artery. It's pretty long, and if it has tension on it for any reason, you know what your body's going to do? It's going to tighten your muscles to prevent you from having a full range of neck motion so that you avoid ripping or putting micro-tears in your carotid. Hence, you won't be able to turn you neck very far, and all the exercises you do to loosen it won't help a bit.

Only with a bodywork technique like strain/counter strain, which takes about two minutes to apply for this particular problem, is the carotid artery going to basically release that strain, and all of sudden you INSTANTLY have a fuller range of motion in your neck and will be able to turn it around. All the exercise in the world wouldn't enable you to do that. Incredible, right? Unbelievable, but I have seen this result several times after the five minute therapy was performed right before my eyes. I've also seen people where, if they get their knee bones reset (which takes about a minute), they can immediately touch their toes where ten years of yoga stretches couldn't enable them to do it. Bodywork is amazing if you know the right techniques and have a good practitioner. If you have an unskillful practitioner, you don't get good results. Only 1-5% of practitioners in any field can ever be considered outstanding, so the odds of finding one are little unless you ask around.

That's the key - you must know the right techniques to use and have access to an experienced practitioner. Rolfing, for instance, works on the muscles and connective tissues, but actually the problem might tighten up again even after it disappears through Rolfing sessions. Basically, muscles surrounding an overstretched artery or vein are going to constrict and become tighter as a defensive mechanism in order to prevent physical movements that might stretch the blood vessels further. Bodyworkers themselves tell me that science doesn't recognize this prioritizing system yet, but they've found it works.

There's an ultra valuable book you can get that visually shows with pictures how to do some of these simple strain/counter strain bodywork corrections on your own body, and martial artists may want to pick it up. It's called "Integrative Manual Therapy for the Autonomic Nervous System and Related Disorder," by Sharon Giammatteo. Most of these bodywork manipulations are really simple, easy to do on someone else, and only take about five minutes apiece. You just look at the book and there are step-by-step instructions on how to do a simple muscular release on someone for a muscle, or internal organ.

These tension-release, strain/counter strain movements basically put pressure on two ends of a muscle or other part of the anatomy, and then squeeze the two ends together so that the tissues can unwind. When you perform this simple form of manipulative release, then all of a sudden muscles that have been locked get a full range of motion again.

I often tell people, once again, that you've got to know that these sorts of healing therapies are available if you want to become the best martial artist possible. This simple method can really help heal muscles and bruises, and that will restore range of movement as well as strength and flexibility. Imagine what it will do for your practice when your shoulder or knee doesn't hurt anymore!

There are all sorts of assists like this that you should know about. For instance, there are things you can do to open up your feet and your hands that you might not normally encounter in a dojo. I could write an entire book or create an entire training course on what to do just to slowly open up the muscles and chi channels in your feet or hands.

For instance, to open up your feet there are tendon stretches (in addition to the basic horse stance which people learn to hold for hours). I also have a piece of equipment called the **Prostretch** that I always use for Achilles tendon stretches, and I also used to use the **Elgin Archxerciser** to create flexibility in the bottom of the foot although you can simply do this with foot rolls themselves. There are **wobble boards**, too, and all sorts of equipment you can train with just for extra flexibility and dexterity. It's important to do everything you possibly can to open up your feet for martial arts.

You can use these inexpensive pieces of equipment, along with the idea of deep practice, to slowly help open up your feet, as well as the skeleton meditation to help open up chi channels to this region. Needless to say, there are things that you could do for your hands as well.

Another issue in martial arts is bruising because people are always getting hurt. They're always getting bruised, and sometimes the body doesn't flush out the internal blood clots in an area that formed in an area that was damaged from sparring. The longer you've been in competitive martial arts, the more likely you've collected injuries that have never quite fully healed until you basically go to a bodyworker or doctor who's going to help you. Egoscue is a wonderful method that can perform healing miracles for this as well.

One of the things you should know is that if you get bruised in martial arts, the homeopathic formula **Arnica Montana** is really good for bruises. It's used by skiers, it's used by Olympians, and it's used by all sorts of sports athletes who experience frequent bruising. It's fantastic.

I've met quite a few Chinese doctors in Taiwan, Malaysia, Hong Kong and China who have deep knowledge of martial arts, since most are practitioners, and who had special formulas I would try for various body ailments. I've tried hundreds of different concoctions from plasters to oils, liniments, supplements, acupuncture, bodywork techniques ... you name it.

I remember I had a Taiwanese herbal and bone doctor make a concoction for me of **raw Tienchi powder together with high grade Korean ginseng**, which I would mix up for myself in New York, and I took this for several months to get rid of internal bruises and blood clots. The important ingredient was the Tienchi powder, so I would have it ground up and take that on its own, too. Later, I just used nattokinase after I discovered its effectiveness.

I had one martial artist/doctor, who used to fight a lot in his youth when he belonged to a Triad gang, tell me that at one time his arm was practically ripped off from a knife fight and he thought he would need an amputation. However, it was Tienchi powder that saved him. You can read a short article about Tienchi powder at www.plantcures.com, and I am anxiously awaiting publication of their book on herbal medicines. I truly believe that every martial artist should become skilled to some degree in bodywork or herbal medicine, and become knowledgeable as to how different martial arts techniques affect the chi of the body. This book starts to give you some simple information along these lines. One should also develop knowledge of true meditation practice, and how the road of martial arts and its techniques can lead to genuine spiritual practices and attainments.

Many people also try to dissolve blood clots in their body through an amazing supplement called **nattokinase**. I'm sure the powers that be will ban it one day not because anything is wrong with it, but because if it became more popular it would make a big dent in the profits of drug companies. In my opinion only one producer for nattokinase is best, and that's the Allergy Research/Nutricology brand.

After you start using it you'll get a slight headache after about 2-3 days because the blood clots are dissolving away inside your veins and arteries and all this extra blood volume is making its way to your brain. Your cranial arteries have not stretched that much in awhile, so for 1-2 days there's a little bit of pressure there until the cranial arteries adjust to a greater elasticity. That, by the way, is how chelation works, too. Chelation helps to remove the calcium and mineral scaffolding that has made arteries inflexible, and once that rigidity is gone, arteries start pumping more blood everywhere. It works because it restores flexibility to arteries. Amazingly, you can now purchase an extremely inexpensive rectal suppository, called **Detoxamin**, to chelate yourself at home.

I've tried dozens and dozens and dozens of different types of therapies to either treat problems in my body or just to see what they would do – hot castor oil packs that penetrate the body to dissolve cysts and adhesions, cupping and scraping to bring out external wind, all sorts of different types of massage therapy, many types of acupuncture, moxibustion, Mongolian knife scraping, visceral massage, *chi nei tsang*, chiropractic manipulation, Chinese bone resetting, cranial sacral work, NMT, IMT, myofascial release, Barnes method, St. John's work, Rolfing, Hellerwork, reflexology, shiatsu, applied kinesiology, neurocranial restructuring, TENS devices, MORA therapy, and so forth. Once you try a bodywork modality, you'll know what it can do for you or others who may be hurt.

I definitely recommend you get exposed to bodywork at a young age because it will help you correct structural abnormalities which in turn, once they are eliminated, enables you to perfect your posture and stances, and knowledge of the various modalities will allow you to pick the right one to help heal injuries and help others such as your sparring partners, students, or friends. If you get hurt in your martial arts practice, it may take many months to heal internal damage unless you know of the proper external and internal therapies and approaches that will help speed the process.

As to sprains and bruises, for many years I used to live in Hong Kong where martial arts of many schools abound, and there are lots of liniments and oils for sprains and bruises on the market from Hong Kong, Malaysia, Taiwan, Indonesia, Burma, Thailand and now China. There's black ghost oil, trauma liniment, XO oil, U-I oil, and so forth. A great book on this topic is "A Tooth from the Tiger's Mouth," by Tom Bisio, which goes into all sorts of therapies and formulations to help the martial artist heal from injuries. Pick it up and keep it handy! Most of these materials can be ordered on the internet, but the cheapest way to buy them is to visit some city with a Chinatown and buy them when you're there.

The other thing I wish to mention on this topic is that the various oils and plasters and other formulations that are coming out of China today are amazing. I could not say that five years ago, but right now, really fantastic formulations are coming out that can really help people in all sorts of ways.

In the Western world, we don't usually stress the use of the oils, liniments and plasters. The closest we usually get is Ben Gay, Icy Hot or Salonpas. When it comes to things like sprains, athletes will often use a supplement like **Wobenzym** or **Vitalzym**, which basically reduce internal inflammation. But really experienced people know how to use all these other treatments, too, and if a locale has had a martial arts tradition for a long time, such as in Hong Kong, you can ask what the dojos are using because people pretty much weed out the bad from the good and use what works.

In any case, the first thing I do if a martial artist comes to me who has been working for years is get a really good chiropractor to work on him. After one or two sessions his bones are realigned and his structure is much better so he can do his forms and stances and movements with much more ease.

If he has any deep injuries or muscular problems, I then send him to get bodywork for his connective tissues. You can start watching a **Z-Health** CD at any time, so I also start him or her on that right away because in as short as a week or two they start getting a fuller range of motion in their joints for better performance, and this helps heal injuries, too. It is strange but true that simple Z-Health exercises helps them achieve a new level of excellence alone, and you can start on these rotational exercises right now even if your body is not perfectly aligned or is in bad shape. In fact, it is used to heal injuries, which is another reason why I so highly recommend it at just a few minutes per day. I can do the whole routine in about ten minutes.

As to supplements, it all depends on the individual, but I usually recommend a detox regime that includes nattokinase in some form or another, and other supplements depending on their personal health situation and the family genes. For instance, if the individual has a health problem of the heart, and the father or uncle or grandparents also had cardio problems, I might put them on a special supplement or set of supplements for heart issues as a preventative and in some cases there are many supplements which actually function as curatives.

Since this is a complicated topic, we'll leave it to the next chapter because what I really want people to do is use supplements mainly for **detoxification**. In terms of standard supplements, the fewer you take the better in life because I like people to get their nutrition from food rather than supplements, unless, as I said, there is a genetic predisposition, in which case a smart person takes some nutritional supplement preventatives that are specific to their situation. For regular people, a multi-mineral multi-vitamin supplement, and perhaps a green powder and/or oil are the most you should be taking, if even that. You might be taking a probiotic for a short period of time, but not always. If you've hurt your joints, there are a number of supplements you can try for pain relief or to help rebuild cartilage, and you will never know which of the many choices will work for you, so buy the highest quality possible to give yourself the best chances of ruling something out.

One manufacturing company with high quality products is **Jarrow** because it's still privately owned. When companies get bought out by large companies, they substitute the high quality ingredients in formulations for lower priced and lower quality, and then things don't work as well. You always see this tendency of quality decline due to the profit motive.

The private owner of a company is usually very proud of his product, however, which is why you tend not to see that problem when they still retain control over their company. Hence, you have great products like A.C. Grace's Ultimate E (best vitamin E on the market), prostate formulas from Beachwood Canyon (www.bcn4life.com), and so on. **Jarrow** and the **NOW** brand (the large orange bottles) don't usually have quality problems, and they're about a third less in price, too. For B-vitamins, the **Freeda** brand is the best in the world, and the **Supernutrition** brand of multi-vitamins is one of the best around.

The topic of supplements is so complicated that it deserves a chapter in itself, so we should approach this topic next.

7

How to Speed Up the Process: Detoxification Supplements for Cleansing the Body

I don't like people taking supplements to build muscle but would rather they build their bodies through a better diet instead. Most muscle supplements are protein supplements, and a lot of times when you take these supplements you bulk up but you lose your chi energy because it all goes into building more muscles. If you want to build a muscular killing frame then that's fine, but if you want an elegant body starting with your natural form, that's usually not the right approach.

The other thing is you will usually get a lot of sexual desire as you take more and more vitamin and herbal supplements because a lot of them are stimulative by nature. And then, of course, if you are a man, you will tend to lose your semen and ejaculate due to the increased sexual desire – either through intercourse or masturbation - and then you won't have sufficient chi to open up your chi channels to get to the *qi-gong* and *nei-gong* stages if you want to get these other extra abilities.

Shakyamuni Buddha, over 2,000 years ago, essentially said, "Look, there are a lot of these guys that have these special abilities. There are actually ten categories of them. After they succeed in their practice, they don't want to be bothered with the human world anymore, and they live well away from regular people in the forests and remote locations. They can live for a long time into the hundreds of years, and from their cultivation have developed a lot of special powers." Even Shakyamuni Buddha told us this.

He also said, "And they usually do this in ten ways." He explained, "Some of the ways are that they eat special herbs, or they eat special foods, or special minerals, or they use special breathing exercises, or special sexual techniques, or try to absorb the energies of the sun or moon, and so on." But he said, "If they don't transform the special foods, minerals, herbs, etc. when they ingest them, and if they cannot transform the energies released because of these special techniques, they can't get to these levels. All these methods also involve mastering mental concentration, but the wrong form of concentration."

In his book, "The Story of Chinese Taoism," my own teacher wrote:

> It is here applicable to explain a problem involving Chinese history. Several emperors and famous individuals of the Han, T'ang, Ming and Ch'ing dynasties who sincerely believed in the Taoist arts and the taking of alchemical drugs such as Han Yu (768-824 A.D.), Su Tung-p'o (1036-1101 A.D.), and Wang Yang-ming (1427-1528 A.D.) brought about their early deaths by ingesting the alchemical drugs of the "fang-shih" of the Taoist School. What was the reason for this? We wish to sincerely warn each of our friends here today who superstitiously believe in modern patent medicines, who take large amounts of tonics, and take special injections of restoratives that they should pay careful attention to this problem.
>
> The "fang-shih" invented and refined mineral drugs made from metals and other substances. In terms of medical and pharmaceutical worth, they made doses for physically treating the human body, and only if suitable doses were applied, not only would it be correct but it would be extremely valuable. However, these types of drugs refined from mineral substances were all irritating in nature, and moreover they acted to fiercely develop physiological functions much like modern vitamins.

The first important point in the methods of ingestion by the *"fang-shih"* orthodox Taoist School is the need to very thoroughly "purify the mind and restrict the passions" in terms of psychological behavior and one can absolutely not be covetous of sexual activities and the consumption of meat before beginning to take the drugs. Otherwise, one will have a very intense tonifying *yang* reaction as soon as the drug is consumed, which will necessarily promote sexual impulses. There is no doubt that this became an amulet for hastening on death by those emperors and famous nobles who spent their days dallying in wine, women and song. This is not at all surprising!

The second important point is that the alchemical drugs consumed by the Taoists required first practicing up to the level wherein the spirit was fixed and the *chi* accumulated, grains were avoided and one did not eat the food cooked in the world of men. Only then could one absorb and fuse the drugs, otherwise one could actually be poisoned by food or die from the ingestion of the drug. In sum, generally those who took alchemical drugs were unable to cut off the desire for "food and sex," but rather, on the other hand, they came to rely upon the effects of the alchemical drugs to realize the pleasures of "food and sex." Then "the taking of drugs to seek immortality contrarily became a misunderstanding of the use of these drugs."

Once again, even you try this approach of special herbs, foods, minerals and supplements, if you don't use this idea of cultivating emptiness or just meditation cultivation in general, you can't transform these elements. You cannot transform your body into the level that's necessary for the *nei-gong* to really commence. You'll definitely experience sexual desires that will lead to your undoing if you don't transcend them.

To be able to use these things to get to the stage of *qi-gong* and *nei-gong*, your mind should be empty and then your yang chi can come up and all the requisite gong-fu can happen naturally. Furthermore, once again you have the barrier of losing your energies too frequently because of sex, and so you can once again see how this intersects with the requirements of the path you must follow if you want to cultivate these higher martial arts abilities.

The *nei-gong* cultivation path is really divorced from the idea of ingesting special formulas or concoctions, including modern supplements. It's really not a path of bulking up at all, or stimulating your chi through any type of substance. It's not a path of intoxication either. Actually, it's really *a path of detoxification*, or elimination of poisons from the body because that's what your yang chi does when it arises. It's poking through your chi channels and pushing out obstructions to the flow of chi, so that your energy meridians fully open, and this is a process of detoxification.

Kundalini or yang chi, when it truly arises, pokes through your body's chi channels to open them. The channels have chi obstructions inside them so that stuff gets pushed out when the yang chi (kundalini) starts circulating everywhere. That's why you feel heat, because you feel the frictional aspect of this clearing process. That's called purification or detoxification in our modern terminology. You're pushing out all these poisons and you get all sorts of phenomena that happen such as summarized in "The Little Book of Hercules" and "Tao and Longevity" or even in "Measuring Meditation."

Hence, what I tell people to do, if they really want to help their martial arts practice, is to take some supplements that help with detoxification. I don't like people buying a lot of supplements because I don't like people buying a lot of things. However, I do like them to try a few things that help with detoxification and cleansing the body.

First, many people take **Candisol**, which is a supplement that will basically kill a lot of the yeast in your body. And you'll notice it within a week or so if you've had Candida because your mind will be lighter and clearer and more empty, and it will be easier to concentrate after you start taking it.

When you have a yeast infection, all the toxins and byproducts that the yeast cells give off get recirculated in your blood. Your liver can't handle these extra detoxification demands so your head gets cloudy, but you get used to that unclarity and think it's natural. If the yeast cells are killed off through Candisol or some other supplement, they're not excreting all this matter again anymore, and your mind tends to become pristine crystal clear ... and you wonder why you never knew it could be this way. It's because you got so used to the unclarity that you didn't even recognize it.

You only need one or two bottles of Candisol to do the job. A bottle is very inexpensive and most people, if they have a Candida yeast overgrowth, can feel the results within a week, sometimes in as short as two or three days. If you have a really strong case of Candida, you might also have to buy a bottle of **Oregacillin Physicians Strength** if your yeast overgrowth problem is serious and take it simultaneously. I used to use Caprylic acid and Thorne Research SF722 to eliminate yeast but this is the approach I now favor. Hence, Candisol is the first gentle thing to try.

I also have people take one or two bottles of any good **glutathione** compound to see if their body experiences any noticeable detoxification reactions. There's Douglas Labs GSH250, Tyler Labs Recancostat and other products with glutathione being developed all the time, such as LivOn Labs' Lypo-Spheric Glutathione where it is encased in nano-spheres as a delivery mechanism. Allergy Research has a new glutathione product as well called acetyl-glutathione.

Glutathione, along with alpha lipoic acid and NAC, are used by your body extensively in the role of detoxification, so this helps your body detoxify harmful chemicals you may have accumulated over time. **Chlorella** helps bind heavy metals for excretion from your system, and **l-glutamine** also helps you heal your stomach lining, intestines and helps detoxify your body, too. There are many detoxification supplements you can try which also help heal and build your body at the same time.

I also tell people that they might want to try a liver or kidney flush and a colonic to help clean the intestines. It's not really too important to me if they don't want to do this right away, but over time, this helps detoxify the body, too. Sometimes the Pekana homeopathic drainage remedies such as **apo-Hepat, Itires and Renelix** can help the body detoxify, too. Those are the big three homeopathics that I use, and Apex Energetics is a good company for specific remedies, too.

A supplement I always favor is 2-3 bottles of **Nature's Pure Body**, because that's the one herbal formulation proven to start clearing out the poisons lodged in your connective tissues. When your yang chi starts arising, all its energies initially don't go into spiritual transformations or anything like that. It just basically goes to cleaning out your chi channels and your body tissues, so anything you can do to help with the initial task of detoxification which also speeds that along as much as possible is a wise strategy. I always recommend Nature's Pure Body together with **Vitalzym** to initially help detox the body.

It's best to *establish a yearly detoxification routine as a habit* because all the poisons you ingest will collect as you age, and produce all sorts of disease and illness as a result if you don't help your body excrete them. If you take one month per year to flush accumulated poisons out of your body, Springtime being a likely candidate, it will produce a big effect in your practice.

Remember, if there's anything else you can do along these lines (supplements, far infrared saunas, colonics, etc.) to help clean out your body and its tissues, the less your energies will be diverted into having to clean out these materials themselves. The quicker you remove accumulated poisons and toxins, the quicker your chi energies can become diverted toward clearing out your chi channels.

At advanced stages of cultivation after your chi channels have been cleared, you usually avoid coarse dredging methods such as colonics and the like because they cause you to lose too much energy. Even overly hot showers will cause you to lose too much energy, and of course you know that about sex as well. So at the upper levels you usually avoid the coarse methods.

At the upper levels it's a matter of not losing energy because your body is more and more composed of pure chi rather than muscular *jing*. Your chi is energy, so you particularly feel the loss. You become very sensitive because of your chi and opened channels, and that's why masters can leave lessons for people who don't feel these things due to the fact that their bodies are clogged up. A lot of people cannot feel anything inside their bodies and think they are healthy whereas it's because their bodies are in terrible shape instead of good condition. These are the type of people who never get sick and then one day they discover they have cancer, and it turns out to be the incurable kind. Those whose channels are open, however, tend to easily get colds, headaches, and the flu due to wind invasions, and that sickness gives their body an opportunity to rev up the immune system and push out all the accumulated poisons.

An important point is not to take stimulants like ginseng and the muscle powders and the bulking agents because you'll feel closed up after using them and they'll also stimulate your sexual desires. That's a big problem, as we've discussed, for higher martial arts practice. Then again, if you have already depleted your sexual energies from too much semen loss, a Chinese formula like **Liu Wei Di Huang Wan** (Beijing Tong Ren Tang is currently said to be one of the best brands, though of course this can change over time) can really help a lot, especially with the kidney and leg channels as you get older. The basic idea is that you don't want to lose too much sexual energy for martial arts practice, and ejaculating semen is called losing the treasure or elixir. If you want your chi channels to open up, you've got to have water in the boiler.

Then again, this doesn't mean, as explained, that you cannot have sex. If a man, you can have a girlfriend-wife-lover, but you should learn the "left hand" Tao school practices which means you must learn how to have sex without ejaculation. You can have sexual intercourse, but you also preserve your energies at the same time. Once mastered, it's actually more pleasurable for both parties, and this type of sexual relations can actually help you open up your channels as well. Most people aren't even introduced to these concepts, which are a blessing to discover if you are young with many more years of active sexual relations ahead of you.

So in summary, the big view is that the martial arts progression is from wai-gong to the qi-gong to the nei-gong, which is internal martial arts practice involving the deep kundalini or yang chi energies of your body, to Tao-gong, which is cultivating spiritual enlightenment.

At the qi-gong stage, where you're just starting to contact the chi energies of your body, you're just making an initial inroad into cultivating your body's chi in conjunction with movement, and in the *nei-gong* stage you progress to the point where the central channel has opened up and all the other energy meridians start opening. Afterwards the higher martial arts become within the realm of reach.

However, you need to cultivate not just chi, but mental emptiness to accomplish those special feats and that comes from meditation practice though you can use anapana or visualization practice to get started. When you sufficiently progress at this level, one of the routes is that you can cultivate all these special powers. It's better at that time to focus on cultivating the Tao but you can also keep doing your martial arts practice at the same time. And that's how you can become an Immortal swordsman or a martial artist with all these special powers.

The martial arts path is basically that you cultivate the body and the mind, and in this case we are saying that to get to the inner energies stage you must be cultivating your mind to discover the pure nature of consciousness, because that level of consciousness purity is connected to the chi purity of your body. You use the body and its energies as a starting point beginning with the cultivation of your muscles through martial arts exercises. You eventually progress to cultivating your internal energies via a route of mental cultivation such as vipassana, visualization, and anapana, and you combine this with your physical practice.

If you cultivate correctly, your body will become healthier, softer and more flexible. Your chi channels will open, your microcosmic (River Chariot) rotation will commence, and you can become an immortal swordsman, immortal martial artist, or whatever. There are all sorts of directions in which you can proceed once you lay the sufficient foundation.

Many schools have this basic sequence. If you go this far, and if you just keep it up with martial arts, then there are many, many things you can do with it. And that's the thing which people should know. I think it's knowledge that you don't usually find in martial arts circles, especially on this topic of internal energy and how to cultivate it, so it's a direction that most people should know about.

Since that basic idea has been communicated, along with all sorts of little known assists to help your practice, it's time for questions.

8
FINAL QUESTIONS AND ANSWERS

John: Well, I think a big thing is, first, this concept of where martial arts fits into the overall path of spiritual transformations, and where the internal physical changes happen during the course of martial arts development is pretty profound. I've been in martial arts for a long time and read much of its literature, and there's not a lot of stuff that really goes into most of these topics. There are only a few books on *nei-gong* and topics like that and none have made the requirements for this clear, or even provided information on how you could help the rest of your ordinary practice.

I guess one of the things that I wanted to ask is the fact that there are teachings out there about playing with your chi and trying to force the chi to move with your mind. And there are all kinds of people who have been taught this sort of material in the sense of the microcosmic and macrocosmic orbits which you mention. They try to make them appear by spinning their chi, as you call it. There are people who are telling you that you should just try and imagine these rotations and mentally try and make them happen by forcing it, by pushing the chi. What would your comment be on that kind of practice and approach to those things?

Bill: I would say this is useless for real *nei-gong*. My teacher always told me this is useless, too, and once you start going through the real gong-fu transformations of *nei-gong* and the opening of the meridians at the level of genuine yang chi and real kundalini energies, rather than playing with surface wind chi, you understand why. That's not the real chi of the body which you are using or affecting. I always listened to him, but I also used to practice that stuff to see for myself and it got me nowhere, just like he said, except for sensations of wind chi in the body which never really open up anything. You can only get minor results from that.

The whole idea is believable, however, because it has a logic and a philosophy behind it, and because it feels like things are opening, but that doesn't make it true. Just because something sounds logical doesn't make it necessary the truth, does it? That is where people go wrong, falling in love with the theory rather than actually achieving any sort of success with this type of practice. Just because it feels open, how can you verify the opening is real rather than just a sensation along that pathway, perhaps outside it or around it?

The loveable idea is that you are taking the physical end results of the path and you're bringing them into the causation of the path. You're bringing this idea of what should happen as a result into the causal mechanism and trying to force that mechanism into producing the result you know about, or expect. You are fruitlessly trying to bring the end results of the path into the causation vehicle of the path thinking that will make things happen quicker. However, what usually happens is that in 999 out of 1,000 cases, or 9,999 out of 10,000 times and so on, people who do this just end up spinning their chi and not getting anywhere.

Can you make puberty occur earlier, and can you pass through it quicker by visualization and the like just because you know what is supposed to happen? No, you cannot. And that's the same problem here in terms of the natural developments within the body.

What you really need to do, rather than visualizing the movements of chi within the body, is focus on stable visualizations where there is non-movement. That is, of course, if you want to use visualizations in your practice. For instance, you don't want to spend your time visualizing the chi moving in areas of your body or in loops around orbits and things of that nature. If you just try to visualize your chakra points with stable one-pointedness, such as visualizing a bright light coming from one of these points wherein you learn how to create a stationary imagination without wavering from the image, that will do more for opening up your chi channels than visualizing chi movements.

Wherever your mind goes your chi will go, so if you hold a focus of imagination on a visualized point within your body, your chi will run to that area and naturally try to open up all the energy channels in the vicinity. That's why you are always told to focus on fixed points rather than moving images when you want to cultivate your chi, channels and chakras. As mentioned previously, the best sort of practice for internal visualizations comes from "The Six Yogas of Naropa: Tsongkhapa's Commentary," which Glenn Mullin authored. Even better as a form of practice is to just keep the mind empty, but I'm always talking about specific techniques so I'm not even discussing emptiness meditation in this book.

Essentially you are concentrating your powers of awareness and focusing them on a single point or region, such as all the bones in your body when you employ the white skeleton visualization technique. When you do that, your mind will settle and your real chi will arise because of the quiet of that concentration. In visualizing your skeleton, your chi will also run to these regions, which helps, and you will be developing the original chi capabilities of your internal physiological functions. There will be natural physical effects within the body that involve the stimulation and movement of energies, but at initial stages this is not really *nei-gong* but just *qi-gong*.

Because you want to train to have your mind empty or stable, since that's when you can tie up consciousness with intent and the physiological chi flows of the body can finally flow uninterrupted, you should cultivate visualization practices on stationary images. When there's only one image in the mind and you're fixated on that image, other wandering thoughts and their associated mental chi flows disappear.

In visualizing movements and playing with body energies, however, you're actually defeating that purpose because thoughts are moving all over the place, wandering here and there once again. That can help you master an outer physical movement, but is that really the correct direction that your energies should go? You think it is, but since the channels aren't open, how do you really know that? You don't! You should focus on a stable image, and let what is supposed to happen just happen, and it will open up the channels.

After they're opened up you can learn to guide the energies if you like, but not before. That's a lower type of practice even though it can produce what you feel are substantial results. Until you unleash your real yang chi by fully opening up your root chakra, *sushumna* and macrocosmic circulations, this isn't the highest you can obtain.

In perfecting a stable imaginary visualization on a point within your body, your chi will eventually mass at that point. And because the chi masses at a particular point, it will open up the chi channels in that vicinity. So if you consider your whole body a hydraulic system of chi channels, then you're concentrating on certain obstructed points to loosen up the whole system, which is why people generally choose specific chakra locations for their visualization practice.

If you concentrate on certain nexus points that are clogged and somewhat free them or loosen them, then all of the sudden they can pop open and the chi will start flowing, sort of like water being released that can then push through the rest of the pipe, so to speak.

If you're concentrating on physical movements and energy movements all the time, however, you're not going to get anywhere in terms of actually initiating those energies. That's why when we get back to the breathing exercises we say you don't count the breaths. You just practice awareness, you witness, as a bodiless mind, that the breath goes in and out. You don't focus on the moving energies, the ins and outs, but just witness it.

You can feel the body and you know its sensations, so it's basically a sensation-observation practice. You can witness that your chi is hot in one area of the body or you feel your energy in another area. And you witness it without pushing, and while keeping your mind relatively empty and free of thought.

The fact that you witness what your chi is like in a region without pressuring it thereby allows it to link up to other chi regions that are disconnected to it. That's how the whole body gets cultivated from this sort of practice. This is also why those people who practice this succeed, rather than the people who push and strain, trying to move their chi here and there or spin it in a meridian orbit they imagine. Your body knows how to link things up, but you don't. You have to create a situation where those energies are given a chance to make the proper linkup without your guidance. Hence, just watch things without pushing. Just let go and remain empty and motionless except for the watching.

This is actually all related to how standing postures initially help open up your chi channels in the body. Your chi channels will start to open when you start to practice the correct form of stance training and remain empty during the exercise! Through stance training in martial arts we are training the physical body. The muscles become stronger, the connective tissues become stronger, and the bones become stronger. Stronger doesn't always mean bigger; however, the muscles do respond with exercise but they don't get pumped up like they would with a body builder. Connecting tissues become more elastic, the bones become hard but the marrow becomes clean of fatty and noxious deposits.

People in the beginning stages of stance training feel pain and develop soreness even in their bones. People feel soreness usually in the thighs, hips and shoulders which can last for any length of time depending on a person's psychological makeup or whether they do the exercises incorrectly. Just a very small change in the position of the posture can produce dramatically different effects in the experience of the practitioner.

While you are standing motionless, the mind during this time is usually going crazy, like a monkey hopping from here to there trying to grab everything. Your mind hurts, your body hurts, and you're thinking this is all crazy ... "what am I doing?" You can't get rid of your thoughts of the feelings and sensations you're going through, and the thought crosses your mind that these things can't be good for you. Your mind even thinks that you are doing yourself harm, and you have all sorts crazy notions running around inside your head. In the beginning you feel pain, and once you identify with that pain, and give up by surrendering to it and letting it happen, then things get better.

Just as surely as the sun sets and a moon arises, you eventually progress from pain to burning, and then to feelings of cold, feelings of itchiness, feelings of fullness and emptiness to feelings of a gentle release and then warmth, and finally a feeling that something larger surrounds your body as you master the position. You stand there and let go, and your chi channels start to open. But first you initially get all these body jerks, and you feel energies running along your nerves. This has been explained as running wind or wind chi. This is a good sign when it occurs, but you must not cling to it. You must just remain aware and return to watchfulness. The uncontrolled movements, the heat, itching, tingling etc. are all just the chi channels trying to open up.

Our energy channels are much like a garden hose that has been pinched where the water is then backed up and only a trickle will come through. Once you open that pinched area on the hose, the water pressure seems to be ten times larger coming out for a minute. The chi channels first offer just a trickle of chi flow, so be prepared for when the dam breaks.

As a matter of fact so many things will happen when the channels open that you will know from this experience that the existence of chi is true, but you must never dwell on any of these experiences but just let them pass without clinging. The more you practice the more you will learn to relax, the more you relax, the less false thoughts will arise and the greater will be your abilities to maintain awareness. The body is healing itself; the chi is starting to flow unobstructed, thoughts ride the chi and where one thinks so does the chi flow. Thinking to put your chi in a certain area at this initial stage is a wrong practice, for as the Taoists always said, "natural spontaneity" is the Tao. You just want the channels to open, and by letting go, while practicing observation and holding the position, the channels will finally start to open.

In the earliest stages of martial arts practice, you just have to let go of holding or pushing your chi, which you're doing every day of your life. You are a bodiless awareness, so if you try to become more like that, that's the one thing that you should take as the result of a path into the causal mechanism that you practice. However, don't try to bring expected chi movements into the causal vehicle of your practice because you don't really know what is supposed to happen. The more you try to be empty but aware and just let go, the more the body will transform to its optimum state of health, whatever that is for the condition of your body at your age and your physical condition.

This is what a lot of people don't understand. There's a philosophy behind all this. There's science behind it. But a lot of people like doing these spinning visualizations of their chi energies running throughout their body because they just want to be doing something. It makes sense. If I just keep visualizing it and try to push my energies, I can definitely feel something after a while. But that's because you're feeling the wind sensations that you've created yourself, but it's never the real chi of the body. The real chi in the body comes up when your mind is empty, which is when the real yang chi arises. When you imagine energies moving in the body, however, this only stirs wind chi in the body, or feelings of internal wind.

Hence, when you do pranayama practices and you get to the stage of pausation, which is called *kumbhaka*, you are actually preparing for internal embryo breathing. When you're meditating your real breathing will often slow down and stop, and it frightens some people, but remaining in that state of pausation – on the outbreath – is a fantastic way to quickly transform your body. Your breath will just stop for 10 seconds or 20 seconds spontaneously. That's when your real yang chi can come up, and people will start feeling a pumping within their lower belly. The Japanese call it *"hara,"* while the Chinese call it the dantien or your lower belly, and you'll feel your real yang chi start pumping at this stage which you can help prepare for by doing pranayama breath holding practices.

It arises when you naturally stop breathing because the root chakra and the sacral chakra are starting to pump. The pumping and chi circulation are called embryo breathing and that's the beginning of the internal stages. In effect, you practice pranayama as a preparatory exercise so that when this pausation eventually happens you don't hold on to it and can maintain that state of non-breathing for as long as possible without using strong effort. Your body's chi is the only thing that knows how to open up your body's channels, and it does it naturally when this non-breathing commences, so you want to cultivate this stage. You can't figure out how to open the channels themselves just by visualizing chi movements within them. It's like going through puberty - you know the general stages but there's no way you can make it happen faster, OK?

John: Right.

Bill: Your body knows what has to happen in what stage, which, and for everybody it's a little different. But it follows the same sort of pattern, which is why I put the general outline in "The Little Book of Hercules," and gave people the four or five practices they should use if they want to cultivate this. You can also find incredibly useful information on this topic in "Tao and Longevity," too.

The big point is that you can't guide it. All you can do is initiate the yang chi into arising from your martial arts practice together with these other cultivation practices that we would say are spiritual. And then it will do all the work itself. You can't speed it up.

Other than to know you should be cultivating these practices, once you start seeing effects you just leave the results to however long it takes. You let the energies released just do what they want to do. It's just like when your teacher tells you to do the horse stance every day and you just hate it. He just tells you to do it every day for months, and a year or two years go by and three years go by and you don't know what's going on. He knows what's supposed to happen but there's no way to speed up the process except by just doing it, and surrendering to the practice.

That's what I mean by deep practice – you just have to do it, and there's no way to speed it up other than to do it correctly as long as you can, in the right way. You just surrender to the process. When doing martial arts you surrender to the practice, and for certain exercises you can try to employ witnessing practice at the same time because that type of detached awareness will help you, too, and allow your chi to more quickly pass through certain regions.

John: Right. And so it seems like the critical points are the practice methods, and then the yang chi has to actually come up, and it has to enter the central channel. And why is that fundamentally important, in terms of opening up all these other channels to develop all these kind of abilities?

Bill: It's just that the physical body has arteries and veins, and we have a nervous system, we have a lymphatic system, and these conduits are spread all throughout our body. We also have an inner subtle body as well, and this inner chi body has its own structure of arteries and veins and distribution networks called the chi channels. Why it has that particular structure, who knows? But it just has that particular structure just as our physical body has its own internal structure, so you take it as a given.

In terms of this structure, the *du mai* and the *jen mai* chi channels start to open up before the *sushumna* does, but after the *sushumna* really opens up you can complete the full opening of the front and back channels and finally feel a continuous circulation of chi in this rotational orbit. Opening the central channel is the key to higher attainments because it goes directly into the brain and along that route are various chakras. There's the belly chakra, there's the heart chakra, and throat chakra and crown chakra, which are directly fed out of that particular channel. And there are entire circulations within the body that can't be opened completely until that channel starts to open.

Once the central channel opens, the chi can start going up that channel and then hits the belly chakra. Then it can go horizontally through all those circuits. And then it can go up higher to the heart chakra, and throat chakra and go through all those connected circuits. In order to open up all the circuits of the body, because you just have to open up all the meridians, the yang chi has to open up all the channels. And why it opens up that one first versus another one, well, I don't know. It's just the body has its own internal structure that must necessitate it, so it just has to open that way. The yoga school even tells you that and of course Tibetan Buddhism says that because Tibetan Buddhism has evolved as a combination of tantric yoga and Buddhist teachings from India, as well as Taoist practices. So it passes along this information, which is actually what occurs.

Other schools will tell you this, too. You can even find this in Western alchemy. The Bible has it in the Song of Solomon. So you can find it everywhere, and it's like going through puberty. Who could have predicted that the human body has something called puberty? Well, who could predict that it has these particular energy pathways, or a natural sequence of channel openings that occur in a certain order and produce particular phenomena?

The big thing is that the opening of the channels, which makes the higher martial arts possible, is a nondenominational phenomenon. Everybody goes through it. It's like weightlifting. If you're Indian, Arab, Chinese, Christian, Muslim, Buddhist, Taoist - or male, female, old, young - it doesn't matter. If you lift weights, you're going to get bigger muscles. This is a nondenominational result, and if you do the right practices you'll get the same nondenominational internal alchemy results which are the basis of the higher martial arts. The topic is complex, so I'm only filling you in on the general structure of the path, and supplying some of the exercises used to accomplish it.

As to how they will ultimately manifest, that's up to you. Will you be a martial artist who wants to be able to jump real high or strike like the wind or who can perform *Dim Mak* just by pointing? Whatever you decide to pursue, once you have your basis or foundation laid, it's all a matter of your training and practice.

Once again, certain natural things are going to come out because everybody has their own natural skills. But it's whatever you trained for. And don't think that what you can't train, that you don't have a skill in a certain area. Because when you just look at the ordinary psychological literature on sports performance, they'll always talk about Olympic athletes who had asthma and polio who became Olympic runners. Gold medal athletes, you know? It starts with motivation, desire or inspiration that is shackled to steady practice in the form of deep practice. So you can achieve anything, you just have to set up the deep practice schedule and start at it.

John: Yeah.

Bill: Even if you have physical problems, you can develop special skills to compensate. I think it was Bruce Lee who had one leg which was a little bit shorter than the other. In order to compensate he learned to emphasize special nuances in his martial arts. I don't remember if that's true or not, but that the whole idea of "The Talent Code" is don't limit yourself if you don't already have a particular ability you want to attain. You can attain all sorts of special skills simply by deep practice.

John: Right.

Bill: And you can see kids, they have these special shoes now, spring board shoes, where they're jumping and doing flips and all that. And it's wonderful, and they're developing all sorts of talents simply because they're practicing day in and day out for hours a day. If you don't practice you'll never get there, but if you do then you can eventually do wondrous things. So that's the big thing.

John: Right. Kind of like that, what's that art? Parkour. I see a lot of street kids doing it. I mean, they do just seemingly amazing things just by practicing. The things kids are doing, once they see it on Youtube or TV now, are just remarkable, remarkable feats.

Bill: At first you see one guy doing something, and then you see ten guys, and then you see one hundred guys, and then one thousand. And you're like, "Oh, it must be just the result of enough practice. It's not talent as much as it is practice to develop talent or skill." And it's the same with skateboarding, surfing or break dancing or anything in that the best performance comes from a tremendous number of individual practice hours. Those tricks are their own type of gong-fu.

This is one of the other reasons why I really wanted to do this book because like I said, I look at America and there are kids that are out there in a cultural wasteland, especially in the Midwest in the heart of football territory, and you want them to be able to have a physical practice where they can use all their energies and develop an athletic skill on their own. You want them to have some area where they can work on improving themselves and develop a skill by themselves, with a skill that's going to last the rest of their life.

Naturally you want them to enter the road of martial arts because it leads to developing internal energies, and then the spiritual mastery of the Tao becomes possible, which is the highest human achievement. If they don't have the road of martial arts they might never encounter knowledge of this path in any other way. It's the only field of athletic self-improvement that acquaints you with the Tao other than possibly yoga, which I've found to be much less useful. It has all sorts of behavioral and mental benefits, to say the least. In any case, you want them to have some athletic skill they can master, and mastery comes down to self-practice for a large number of hours, and then this rule applies to martial arts.

You're not going to be playing football when you're age sixty or seventy. You might be watching it on TV but you won't be playing the rough sports, and that's what's wrong with our athletic focus in today's educational system. But you can still be doing martial arts your whole life and as you get older, your skills will continue to get better, too. You cannot say that for the professional sports like football. Furthermore, you can always be doing the internal energy aspect to it that leads to *Tao-gong*.

I wanted to put this path understanding into this really tiny book so that these young guys know, "Oh, my god. If I just start doing my martial arts and do this stuff with a devoted practice schedule, knowing about this 10,000 hour thing, I'll start making progress and I'll get this world class gong-fu." If I was a young guy again I'd really want to know this, but this information wasn't available when I was young so I wanted to make it available along with the idea of "deep practice" and why it works.

What I really wanted to do is offer that or interject this information into American or Western culture or any place this might take hold. Because after you have this information available for 100 or 200 or 300 years, wherein people have been practicing it, then lots of people will be developing schools on internal martial arts, and you'll have new individuals arising like the Eight Immortals of Taoism, and you'll have laid a good foundational basis for the Tao to take hold in society. It's a sad statement that people only tend to believe things after they see superpowers and the like.

It's often the Esoteric school that lays the foundation for higher Mind-Only cultivation to be able to arrive in a region simply because it's materialistically based, and people like that and then can believe the claims of self-cultivation because they can see the materialistic results. If youngsters can grow up in an area where you already have this rich tradition that has taken hold, then they can still make progress according to the principles because they're finally everywhere.

John: Right.

Bill: But the key today in martial arts is that students don't know this idea of practice of 10,000 hours in depth, with the nuances, or this idea that you don't initially need great talent to become a great martial artist. You just need the right effort, practice correctly according to a deep schedule, and visualization helps. If you match your movement efforts with breathing, and when you start feeling your chi, that's what that chi internal energy stuff is all about. That's a whole pathway, and if you want to go there, you can do this. You can go and you can use these things, and then you can get all these special abilities if you work hard enough and make the breakthrough. The key is that young guys, who have the most virility and time to put into this, didn't have this information previously, so I wanted to make it available.

It still takes training and practice. And the key to that which is the big thing that plagues most men, not women, is the celibacy aspect, and how to handle sexual desires and still become a great martial artist whose channels all open and whose chi purifies. I had to mention that because you need to know what can possibly defeat you along this route. If you're missing this information, if you're missing this one link in the entire chain and the knowledge on how to handle it, you're going to be wondering why in the world it's not working for you.

Basically, there are a lot of things I hoped you learned about from this short book. First there is the idea of *wai-gong, qi-gong*, and then *nei-gong* and *Tao-gong*. The idea is that your martial arts practice must proceed to the level of *nei-gong*, or internal energy cultivation, rather than just remain at a superficial level of *qi-gong*, which is the way to break a plateau. There are many ways to get to *nei-gong*, but the two most common routes involve anapana/pranayama, and visualization practices.

Visualization practices of movements can help you perfect your outward form, but the visualization of stable images is what cultivates your chi. Basically, when you cultivate an empty mind of mental stability, your yang chi will arise and start clearing your chi channels of obstructions. This will produce marks and signs, known as gong-fu, and when you finally have opened up the *sushumna* central channels, and started the River Chariot and full macrocosmic and macrocosmic circulations, you are on the road to *nei-gong*. That's when special abilities will arise.

As to the idea of peak performance in martial arts and getting to the level of world class excellence, you have to pick up the book "The Talent Code," and read what it has to say, and then use those insights to help you schedule your practice. I've even mentioned the three movies I really like young kids to see that hammer home this idea of the necessity of practice to become a world class level expert. When you lose motivation, you can view them over and over again.

Naturally you're going to hurt yourself along the way, so I've given some hints of bodywork and supplements that you usually don't find in martial arts circles either, and some equipment you can use to specifically cultivate your feet, which is really important because it's difficult to open up the chi channels into your feet. All these things are related to a larger topic of cultivating and perfecting your physical body, so they're appropriate. As to supplements, I want you to think of their use in terms of detoxification rather than muscle development if you really want *nei-gong*.

All in all, I simply wanted people to have the information I did not have when I was in my twenties or teens, when this would have been of the greatest use to me. But even if you're older, all this information can still help you, and I'm hoping there are quite a few things you picked up to help you excel in your martial arts practice and take it to the next level.

And if you want more information, once again I suggest you go to MeditationExpert.com and download many of our free materials on *nei-gong*, or look for our other books on Amazon.com.

OTHER BOOKS OF INTEREST

If you enjoyed this work, you may find some of these other books helpful. Most are available on amazon.com while some are only available at the site www.meditationexpert.com:

- *Spiritual Paths and their Meditation Techniques*, William Bodri and Nan Huai-chin (Top Shape Publishing, Nevada, 2010).

- *Twenty-Five Doors to Meditation: A Handbook for Entering Samadhi*, William Bodri and Lee Shu Mei (Red Wheel/Weiser, Maine, 1998).

- *Tao and Longevity: Mind-Body Transformation*, Nan Huai-chin and Wen-Kuang Chu (Weiser Books, Maine, 1984).

- *Working Toward Enlightenment: The Cultivation of Practice*, Nan Huai-chin (Red Wheel/Weiser, Maine, 1993).

- *To Realize Enlightenment: Practice of the Cultivation Path*, Nan Huai-chin (Weiser Books, Maine, 1994).

- *How to Measure and Deepen Your Spiritual Realization*, William Bodri and Nan Huai-chin (Top Shape Publishing, Nevada).

- *The Little Book of Hercules*, William Bodri (Top Shape Publishing, Nevada, 2011).

- *Your Destiny is in Your Own Hands*, William Bodri (Top Shape Publishing, Nevada, forthcoming 2012).

- *I am That: Talks with Sri Nisargadatta Maharaj*, Nisargadatta Maharaj (Acorn Press, North Carolina, 1990).

- *Be as You Are: The Teachings of Sri Ramana Maharshi*, Sri Ramana Maharshi and David Godman (Arkana, London, 1985).

Made in the USA
Lexington, KY
01 June 2013